DAOISM IN CHINA

DAOISM IN CHINA

AN INTRODUCTION

BY WANG YI'E
TRANSLATED BY ZENG CHUANHUI
EDITED BY ADAM CHANZIT

FLOATING WORLD EDITIONS

FIRST EDITION, 2006

PUBLISHED BY FLOATING WORLD EDITIONS, INC.
26 JACK CORNER ROAD, WARREN, CT 06777
BY SPECIAL ARRANGEMENT WITH
CHINA INTERCONTINENTAL PRESS, BEIJING, CHINA.

ISBN 1-891640-39-9

LIBRARY OF CONGRESS CATALOGING-IN-PUBLICATION DATA AVAILABLE

Translators' Preface

Daoism is considered by many scholars to be the least understood of the world's major religions. In fact, many Westerners do not realize that Daoism *is* a religion. Daoism is more familiar to most in terms of the "philosophy" of Laozi and Zhuangzi, but considerably less so concerning the cultural, social, and historical framework surrounding their thought. The study of Daoism as a religion is especially useful in understanding the Daoist school of philosophy as well as Chinese spirituality in general. Its study may also lead to the realization that prevalent conceptions of "philosophy" and "religion" are perhaps too narrow and need to be broadened when looking cultures such as that of China.

The cooperation in translating and editing this book between a Chinese and American scholar has been an enlightening experience. Translating from Chinese (especially classical Chinese) to English is a difficult task and requires numerous careful and wise choices on the part of the translator. One choice we made, for example, concerns translating names of Daoist sects, mountains, temples, and deities. We opted to translate some names directly into English if we thought they were plausible and helpful to a reader; however, sometimes there really is no good, simple translation of a mountain or deity, and simply using the accepted *pinyin* romanization at least does not mislead (this practice is somewhat standard in working with Indian Buddhism). On a deeper level, it is important to note that in classical Chinese, one Chinese character often has multiple meanings, allowing for ambiguity crucial to Daoist rhetoric; often when translating these texts into English, the meaning becomes too specific, too narrow. The translator then must find a way to best express the original meaning (or meanings), but when it comes to translating from classical Chinese into English, much is inevitably "lost in translation." Furthermore, this book was originally written for a Chinese audience, and in the original Chinese edition many sections assume cultural and historical knowledge that an average, educated Westerner would not be aware of. Therefore we often added a sentence or two in order to clarify some points.

The first three chapters help situate Daoism within the context of Chinese history and trace its development. This is probably the most crucial section of the text for someone seeking a brief answer to the question: "What is Daoism?" The contents of the fourth chapter regarding Daoist deities cannot be fully retained with one casual read; hopefully interested readers, however, will develop a sense of the Daoist pantheon. The fifth and sixth chapters contain detailed information concerning sacred temples and mountains. While the information may be in too much detail for some readers, it could be of interest to those wishing to travel in China. In fact, visitors to Daoist temples or sacred Daoist mountains might find it a handy guide.

The final three chapters convey a sense of the state of Daoism today. It is important to realize that much of the Daoist intellectual tradition as well as its cultivation techniques are transmitted from master to disciple, while its more popular movements flourish outside of big cities. Therefore knowledge of major organizations and their activities does not equate to a complete understanding of the scope of contemporary Daoism. Readers may particularly be interested in the section in the final chapter concerning the influence of Daoism on traditional Chinese festivals.

More than anything else, we hope this book will pique readers' continued interest in Daoism, whether through further reading, climbing one or all of the five sacred mountains, or even cultivation and practice. As the modern literary giant Lu Xun once remarked, "Daoism is the root of Chinese culture." The study of Daoism is an excellent way to penetrate the deep, ancient traditions of Chinese thought, and is also a source of much wisdom which can broaden our conceptions of the world and aid us in our daily lives. Happy reading.

Zeng Chuanhui and Adam Chanzit
Members of the World Religions Institute
Chinese Academy of Social Sciences, Beijing, PRC

Ed. note: While Dao, Daoist, and Daoism are now the correct *pinyin* spellings of these terms, Tao, Taoist, and Taoism have have been used to refer to the proper names of publications and organizations that retain the older Wade-Giles romanization.

INTRODUCTION

When writing an introduction to Chinese religion, one must first discuss Daoism, because it is the only religion to have adopted the spiritual traditions of early China. China is a multiethnic nation with many religions. Among the five major religions existing in modern times—Daoism, Buddhism, Catholicism, Protestantism, and Islam—only Daoism is indigenous. The cosmology of Daoism is consistent with that of ancient Chinese philosophy; its principles—including worship of nature, striving for inner purity, and reduction of personal desire—have been important aesthetic goals for Chinese people for tens of centuries. Daoist images, from paintings to literature of the sublime realms and the immortals inhabiting them, have spread throughout China and have been passed down from generation to generation. These traditions have become so widespread that much of the content of Daoist belief has evolved into common practice and is seen as folk custom. Foreign religions that have come to China have thus inevitably been influenced by Daoism, even as they penetrate Chinese culture.

Religious Daoism was officially born in the second century CE. It originally appeared as a revolt by the oppressed peasantry, who imagined an ideal, just society. However, it was later molded by religious reformists such as Gehong, Lu Xiujing, and Wang Chongyang, and enjoyed its most prosperous period from the 7th to the 14th centuries, becoming, along with Confucianism and Buddhism, one of the three ideological pillars of medieval China. After the 15th century, the mutual influence between the three ideologies increased, blurring distinctions between them. Many

people believe in both Buddhism and Daoism, and there are also many common practices that incorporate values and concepts from both traditions, as well as Confucianism. Temples and worshippers that are purely Daoist have decreased in modern times, yet the influence of Daoism on Chinese culture remains profound. To this day, there are tens of thousands of Daoist monks, clerics and nuns, and around two thousand and five hundred temples. Many Daoist temples are not only sacred places of worship, but also tourist attractions with great historical and cultural value, representing essential traits of Chinese civilization.

This concise introduction to Daoism, authored by Professor Wang Yi'e and published by Floating World Editions in cooperation with Intercontinental Press, offers an overall introduction to the origin, formation, and evolution of Daoism, including information about its doctrines and systems, the compilation of its classics and scriptures, as well as its influence throughout the world. The work not only provides a reader with a basic introduction to Daoism, but also will be helpful in better understanding China and its people.

It is my sincere wish that many readers enjoy this book.

Zhao Kuangwei
Center for Religious Research
China

STELE DEPICTIING DIAGRAMS OF THE FIVE SACRED MOUNTAINS, AT ZHONG YUE SHAN, THE CENTRAL SACRED MOUNTAIN.

CHAPTER I

SPIRITUALITY IN EARLY CHINA

Among the existing five major religions in China—Buddhism, Daoism, Islam, Catholicism, and Protestantism—only Daoism is indigenous to China. Although of these five religions Daoism currently has the least number of temples, its influence on the development of Chinese culture and the daily habits of Chinese people has been the greatest, precisely because it has inherited and carried on the earliest spiritual traditions of China. In any corner of the world inhabited by Chinese, one can easily see the influence of Daoism. In fact, it is no exaggeration to say that Chinese culture cannot be understood without a proper understanding of Daoism.

The religious Daoist order was formed in the second century, during the Later Han dynasty (25–220). However, its doctrine and patterns of thought can be traced back to many centuries before the Christian era. It is commonly accepted that religious Daoism has three major origins: 1) Nature and ancestral worship originating in primitive society; 2) the doctrines of immortals, the ancient mystics (*fangshi*) and their occult techniques (*fangshu*) emerging in the Spring and Autumn and Warring States Periods (roughly 8th to 3rd centuries BCE); and the 3) Huang-Lao School, which flourished in the Han dynasties, from 202 BCE to 220 CE. Huang signifies

Huangdi, the Yellow Emperor, the legendary founder of China, while Lao signifies Laozi, author of the well-known *Daode Jing* (*Tao Te Ching*) and one of many philosophers later termed Daoists.

YUAN DYNASTY RELIEFS OF DAOIST SUBJECTS. DAOCHUAN COUNTY, SHAANXI PROVINCE.

NATURE AND ANCESTRAL WORSHIP
IN PRIMITIVE SOCIETY

Daoism is a polytheistic religion, many of the traditions and doctrines of which were inherited from people who lived in the land now called China. Nature and ancestral worship are beliefs in the spirits of nature and the souls of deceased tribal ancestors. According to archaeological data, the earliest religious consciousness in China appeared in the late Paleolithic age, from one hundred to fifty thousand years ago. In 1933, when archaeologists found bones of Upper Paleolithic cave men at a place called Mount Dragon Bone (where so-called Peking Man was originally discovered), they were astonished to notice that all the skulls were placed in the same direction, and that stone spinning wheels and arrowheads were buried with the skeletons. Traces of red iron ore, which could only be obtained from a place several kilometers away, were scattered around the tomb. Yet no such funerary objects were found in fossil sites from earlier periods, indicating that these cave dwellers were the first to have some concept of a world beyond death.

Numerous archaeological excavations and historical records have demonstrated that the origin of nature worship was directly related to the initiation of agricultural activities. In early times, when agricultural technology was still basic, harvests heavily depended on fluctuations of the natural environment. People ascribed every kind of natural phenomenon to various controlling deities, linking all natural changes to the spiritual. If an abundant harvest came, it was a reward from the deities of the natural world;

if there were a poor harvest, it was punishment from the spiritual world. Since weather had such a powerful influence on the product of farmers, the sky or "heavenly" realms were seen as unfathomable and omnipotent. The sun was also commonly worshiped, because it gives light and heat, symbolizes the shift between day and night, and is also related to the four seasons. Due to their vital influence on agricultural activity, other natural elements were also worshiped, such as the earth, moon, stars, wind, thunder, rivers, lakes, seas, plants, and animals. The totem symbols of celestial bodies have been found on sites of excavated relics from the Neolithic age, such as Dawenkou Cultural Site, Tai'an, Shandong; Hemudu Cultural Site, Yuyao, Zhejiang; and the Majiayao Cultural Site, Lintao, Gansu.

Ancestral worship was predominant in Chinese tradition, probably because in ancient times people had no way to prevent droughts and floods, necessitating the unification of all tribes under the leadership of powerful rulers who were later viewed as heroic. Since these heroes were also considered ancestors, this laid the foundation for the Chinese tradition of ancestral worship. Legendary hero-ancestors such as Fuxi and Nuwa, the Three August Ones, and the Five August Emperors, are the earliest figures of this sort. Hero-ancestor worship was later extended to all extraordinarily talented and virtuous figures found in history, including emperors, ministers, generals, scientists, doctors, or other benefactors. This tradition has also resulted in special emphasis on the virtue of filial piety and burial of the dead, including burying precious belongings with the dead as offerings. As it turns out, this custom helped create rich archaeological resources.

In the Shang dynasty (roughly 2000 to 1000 BCE), primitive totem and nature worship were replaced by the worship of Heaven (Shangdi) and sacrifice to ancestors. The deities who were believed to represent the will of Heaven were called *shen,* or gods, and the spirits of the dead ancestors of families and clans were called *gui,* or ghosts. Those who played the role of bridge between deities and humans were called *wu,* a male witch, or *xi,* a female witch. The great quantity of excavated material from this period proves that divination was performed using bones and tortoise shells. Divination was usually practiced in anticipation of important events, such as wars, sacrifices, hunts, or farming decisions. Oracles were used to foretell the nature of harvests, offspring, wealth, weather, and stockbreeding.

The Zhou dynasty (1100–256 BCE), which replaced the Shang, inherited its spiritual traditions. Celestial and royal powers became even more closely linked; not only did the emperors' orders come from Heaven, but they themselves were believed to be "Sons of Heaven." They were thought to rule the mundane world in accordance with a "Heavenly Mandate." A strict ritual system stipulated that only Sons of Heaven had the right to sacrifice to all deities. Dukes, on the other hand, might sacrifice to heaven and earth, the sun, moon, and constellations, and the mountains in their own dukedoms, while the common people were allowed to sacrifice only to their own ancestors. Historical records of the sacrificial systems, as well as punishment via disease and disaster due to violations, can be found in such classics as the *Book of History* (*Shi Jing*), the *Book of Ritual* (*Li Zhi*), and the *Rites of Zhou Dynasty* (*Zhou Li*).

Additionally, in the process of founding its religious order, Daoism synthesized many nature and ancestral deities, along with their sacrificial ceremonies, from many minority groups of southwest China.

According to *A Handbook of Daoism* (Zhongzhou Ancient Works Publishing House, Henan, China, 1993), Daoist deities may be classified into eight groups based on their origins: 1) those who evolved from the totem and nature worship of various clans in ancient China; 2) those who evolved from ancestor, hero, and sage worship; 3) those of the five sacred mountains (Mount Tai in Shandong, Mount Heng in Hunan, Mount Hua in Shaanxi, Mount Heng in Shanxi, and Mount Song in Henan) and the four sacred rivers (Yangtze River, Yellow River, Huai River, and Jishui River) who came into being during the early stages of the unification of Chinese society from the 3rd century to the 1st century BCE; 4) those of heaven, earth, the four directions, and towns and villages, who came into being during the middle of the Han and Tang dynasties from roughly the 3rd century to the 9th century; 5) The Three Pure Ones (the supreme deities, Daoist deities of unfathomable height) and Four Imperials (the three emperors and one queen who rule the heavenly domain) who came into being during the later unified society period; 6) the deities absorbed from Buddhism; 7) the local, folk, and trade deities taken from various areas and nationalities; 8) the sect founders, great masters, immortals who gained eternal life and godlike powers through cultivation, and many famous hermits accumulated over Daoist history.

Thus it can be seen that the pantheon of Daoist deities contains many from the earliest times, as well as those who earned their membership in later chapters of the religion's history.

Doctrines of Immortals and Occult Masters in the Spring and Autumn and Warring States Periods

The doctrines of immortals also arose from ancient nature and ancestral worship. These doctrines not only propose that there are spirits in our everyday environment as well as spirits of deceased ancestors, but also that people can discover medicines which can prevent death. People can cultivate longevity and gain supernatural powers by consuming elixirs. Once they become immortal, they enjoy a life free of confinement, discontent, and earthly concerns. They can also roam freely between heaven and earth.

These immortal doctrines were quite popular during the Warring States period (475–221 BCE), and many descriptions of immortals can be found in books from northern and central China from that time. For example, in the *Zhuangzi*, written by the philosopher Zhuang Zhou, immortals were classified as *shenren* (godlike person), *zhiren* (supreme person), or *zhenren* (perfected person). In the first chapter, "Free and Easy Wandering," Zhuang writes: "There is a godlike person living on faraway Guye Mountain, with skin like ice and snow, gentle and shy like a young girl. He doesn't eat the five grains, but inhales the wind, drinks the dew, soars on the clouds and mist, rides a flying dragon, and wanders beyond the four seas."

Another famous ancient book, The *Classic of the Mountains and Seas (Shanhai Jing)*, claims there is a sacred mountain named Kunlun somewhere in northwest China. It contains splendid palaces, beautiful gardens, various precious flowers, fantastic trees, rare birds, and bizarre beasts. The water flowing from the sacred spring could make people live forever. The original ancestors of the Chinese, including the Yellow Emperor and Empress Lei, along with Great King Yu (a hero-ancestor) and the Queen Mother of the West (the head of all goddesses) reside there.

The *Liezi,* another ancient classic, records that there are five sacred mountains in a place named Guixu, beyond the East China Sea. They are called: Daiyu (Vehicle of Mount Tai), Yuanqiao (Round Mountain), Fanghu (Square Kettle), Yingzhou (Sea Island), and Penglai (*peng* and *lai* are names of grasses). The height and perimeter of each mountain is 15,000 kilometers, the perimeter of the plains on the peaks is 4,500 kilometers, and the distance across all the islands is 35,000 kilometers. Houses, pavilions, and terraces there are made of gold and jade. The birds and beasts wear silk robes. Pearls, flowers and fruit grow on the trees, and anyone who eats of them will never die. Immortals live on the mountains. Their voices echo each other for long distances; they fly up and down, visiting each other. The population is countless.

MING DYNASTY GLAZED PLAQUE, QUEEN EARTH TEMPLE. JIEXIU COUNTY. SHANXI PROVINCE.

In his great *Records of the Historian (Shi Ji),* Sima Qian, the foremost historian of the Han dynasty, gives a more complete description. He relates the stories of how kings and vassals sent expeditions in search of the three legendary sacred mountains of Penglai, Fangzhang (Fanghu), and Yingzhou. It was told that they were located in the Gulf of Bohai, which was not so distant, and there one could supposedly find pills of immortality. From a distance, the mountains seemed to be clouds; but when within reach, they were submerged in water. Whenever the shores were about to be accessed, the mountains were blown away, or the boats swept back. Hence the mountains were actually untouchable.

There are many other classics telling similar tales: the immortals are those with great power, who need not strive or labor, and are free of disease and death. They dance, sing, or drink all day. They dwell in the places where *yin* and *yang* are perpetually harmonious, the sun and moon always shine, seasons are punctual, wind and rain is balanced, boys and girls grow healthy and tall and find suitable mates, and harvests are abundant.

As in other cultures, the quest for immortality was a pastime chiefly of kings and nobles, who had the motivation and means to pursue it. Their courts in turn attracted the attention of mystics called *fangshi* (*fang* means outlying area, *shi* means learned person; *fangshi* arose from outside society), who claimed to have special skills and knowledge of divination, astrology, and medicine, or knew the secret ways to the sacred mountains. These skills were called *fangshu* (*shu* means technique).

In the beginning, *fangshi* and *fangshu* were rather broad and general terms because the distinction between science and magic was not understood. Astronomy and astrology, chemistry and alchemy, medication and exorcism, any knowledge or practice that was arcane or unusual was classified as *fangshu,* and those expert in them were labeled *fangshi.* However, the two terms in historical records refer mostly to the self-claimed masters of immortality; among them, Changhong, Pengzu, Rongcheng, Xufu, Li Shaojun, and Luanda, were especially famous. In particular, the story of Xufu's journey to the sacred mountains is well-known in China and Japan.

It is said that Xufu was a *fangshi* during the Qin dynasty (221–206 BCE). After he succeeded in convincing the Emperor of Qin (China's first emperor) to sponsor his expedition, he was sent, along with thousands of virgin boys and girls, to seek pills of immortality supposedly located in sacred mountains across the sea to the east. But he never returned, leaving an unsolved mystery. Daoism inherited the idea that people could use pills of immortality to become immortals or spirits, and this had great influence over the core beliefs of early Daoists. Over time, Daoism developed and expanded religious customs and doctrines, with what are called "outer alchemy" and "inner alchemy" playing central roles and becoming important and unique techniques of *xiulian,* or self-cultivation.

HUANG-LAO DAOISM IN THE HAN DYNASTY

The spiritual elements of Daoism were adopted from nature and ancestral worship, and doctrines of the immortals, while its intellectual side came from philosophical Daoism and Huang-Lao Daoism. Daojia or "philosophical Daoism" is the title used since the Han dynasty for the school founded by Laozi and Zhuangzi, great philosophers of the earlier Spring and Autumn and Warring States Periods. According to the *Records of the Historian* of Sima Qian, Laozi was born around 570 BCE, in Ku County in the state of Chu. Because the characters for Lao and Li were pronounced identically at that time, his surname was mistakenly recorded as Li in many historical records. It is said Lao was the royal historian of the Zhou dynasty, who, having witnessed the disintegration of the dynasty in his old age, resigned from his duties at the court to become a hermit. Zhuangzi was the major philosophical successor to Laozi's doctrine. Although the dates of is life are also impossible to verify with certitude, he is believed to have lived from around 355 to perhaps 275 BCE.

Dao is the core concept of Laozi's philosophy. It is the root and essence of all that exists in the universe, and is also the origin of the universe. In the *Daode Jing,* or *Classic of Dao and Its Virtue,* it is written that: "Dao emerged before the cosmos. It is solitary, self-grounded, and unchanging, permeating all processes without fail. We can deem it the mother of the world. Look at it and you will not see it, listen to it and you will not hear it. It is shapeless, existing apart from the senses. It is the permanent root from which all things grow."

Zhuangzi expanded on the philosophy of Laozi in his book, *Zhuangzi*. He stated that Dao is actual and real, not something imagined. Although it cannot be directly perceived, it permeates everything at all times. It is permanent and infinite, and its movement is limitless. The birth, changes, and extinction of all things have a temporary nature, yet through their changes they manifest the working of Dao. Zhuangzi further explains the doctrine that Dao accomplishes all this through *wu wei*. Although literally meaning "non action," *wu wei* is a crucial concept in Daoist philosophy and religion, and in fact advises that one should not act according to artificial rules, norms, and values, but instead should act in accordance with the principles of Dao. Zhuangzi also states that the nature of Dao is supremely good; it produces all things in their natural manifestations, without any idea of realizing any benefit for its deeds, the essence of *wu wei*. Dao is of the same essence as people, because it is immanent, so the spiritual changes experi-

TANG DYNASTY STATUE OF LAOZI.

enced by people express the Dao. He concludes that people are of the same essence as everything in the world: "Heaven and Earth were born at the same time I was, and the ten thousand things are one with me."

Laozi's doctrine merged with that of Huangdi in the scholastic fellowship of the Jixia Academy at Linzi (now Zobo in Shandong), the capital city of the state of Qi during the Warring States period. The so-called Huang-Lao School is the general name for those who advocated this form of Daoism. They honored Huangdi and Laozi as the founders of their school, and by linking the two they symbolically elevated its status. They also absorbed some Confucianist, Moist, and Legalist thought. Their surviving representative works are the "Nine Lords" ("*Jiuzhu*") now a chapter in *Yiyin,* and *The Four Books of Huangdi.*

In the early years of the Former Han dynasty, the economy of the empire had been damaged severely by long, drawn out wars. In order to reinvigorate and rehabilitate the nation, some ministers such as Zhangliang and Caocan proposed Huang-Lao Daoism as a theory of statecraft. In his book *Xinyu* (*New Discourses*), the scholar Lujia devoted a full chapter to explain non-action, extolling *wu wei* as the most distinctive feature of the Dao of Huangdi and Laozi. He concluded by presenting historical precedents, claiming that the policies of Emperor Yao and Shun in primitive times, and those of the more recent Regent Zhou, ostensibly seemed quite passive, but in the end made the whole society prosperous and peaceful. The First Emperor of Qin dominated the country with despotic policies and military force, but his reign

THE YELLOW EMPEROR INQUIRES ABOUT DAO.
THE YELLOW EMPEROR IS REGARDED AS THE FOUNDER OF CHINESE CIVILIZATION. THIS PICTURE RELATES THE STORY OF HOW, AFTER UNITING THE MIDDLE KINGDOM OF CHINA AND BRINGING PEACE AND PROSPERITY TO ITS PEOPLE, THE YELLOW EMPEROR TRAVELED TO MOUNT KONGDONG. THERE HE VISITED GUANGCHENGZI, AN EARLY DAOIST MASTER, TO EXPRESS HIS DESIRE TO INFUSE CROPS WITH THE VITAL ENERGIES OF HEAVEN AND EARTH, AND SO PROVIDE FOR THE NEEDS OF THE PEOPLE THROUGH THE CONTROL OF YIN AND YANG.

quickly crumbled. It is stated in the *Records of the Historian* that when Caocan was Prime Minister, he respected Gaigong, an expert on Huang-Lao Daoism, as the most honored of his officials. Caocan managed the country according to Huang-Lao Daoism, brought peace and wealth to the country, and was praised as the "Sage Prime Minister."

In the reigns of Emperor Wen and Jing (179–141 BCE), productivity developed quickly under the guidance of Huang-Lao Daoism, which promulgated purity and non-action. Queen Dou, wife of Emperor Wen and mother of Emperor Jing, in particular

LAOZI TERRACE AT THE TRADITIONAL HOMETOWN OF LAOZI. LUYI COUNTY, HENAN PROVINCE.

advocated Huang-Lao Daoism. The emperor, prince, and other royal relatives assiduously studied the writings of the Huang-Lao School and this philosophy dominated the times.

It was during the time of Emperor Wu, the son of Emperor Jing, that Huang-Lao Daoism became the theoretical foundation of belief in immortals. Although also an advocate of Confucianism, Emperor Wu (140–87 BCE), was entranced by various doctrines of immortals. The advocates of these doctrines were eager to establish a theoretical system that could be used to support their opposition to Confucianism, and naturally looked to the apparently

THE SERMON TERRACE OF LOUGUANTAI, WHERE LAOZI IS BELIEVED TO HAVE TRANSMITTED THE TEACHINGS OF THE *DAODE JING* TO YINXI. SHAANXI PROVINCE.

Six Gods of the Southern Constellation. Ming dynasty fresco, Jia County, Shaanxi Province.

more "mystical" Huang-Lao Daoism. On the one hand, texts of the widely prevalent Huang-Lao Daoism contained such expressions as "The Dao of everlasting sight and eternal life," which could be adapted for their use. On the other hand, only Huangdi and Laozi had stature that could match that of Yao, Shun, and Confucius. Hence various precepts of Huang-Lao Daoism were gradually applied to the doctrines of immortals, and the two systems eventually merged into one. This system of thought ended up as the foundation of a religion independent of philosophical Daoism, in which the founder Laozi was promoted to the Heavens and crowned as an immortal, a deity.

During the Later Han dynasty (25–220 CE), Buddhism was introduced into China from India, and Laozi was worshiped along with its founder, the Buddha of our era, Shakyamuni. According to the *History of the Later Han Dynasty* (*Hou Han Shu*), Emperor Huan (132–167 CE) believed in immortals. In 165, delegates were sent to Ku County in Henan Province, the hometown of Laozi, to perform sacrificial rites in memory of Laozi. The next year, the emperor himself offered a sacrifice to Laozi in Zhuolong Palace. Laozi was depicted as the manifestation of Dao, a supreme god who created and coexists with the universe.

However, these beliefs in immortals only existed in the form of the thoughts and imaginations of individuals; no organizations and congregations promoting or subscribing to them had been established. Though they had been theoretically systematized, these doctrines were only popular beliefs, mixed with other ancient cultural components without obvious distinction. Therefore they could not at this time be regarded as a fully formed religion.

Song dynasty iron guardian at Chongsheng gate, Zhong Yue Temple. Henan Province.

CHAPTER 2

THE ESTABLISHMENT OF DAOIST ORGANIZATIONS AND THE LINEAGE OF THE CELESTIAL MASTERS

THE RISE OF EARLY DAOIST ORGANIZATIONS

Religious Daoism officially came into being in the 2nd century, near the end of the Later Han dynasty. Historians mark the founding of religious Daoism with the creation of the so-called Five Bushels Sect (Wudoumi Dao—anyone wishing to join had to agree to pay a tithe of five bushels of rice) by Zhang Daoling and the Supreme Peace Sect (Taiping Dao) by the three brothers Zhangjiao, Zhangbao, and Zhangliang. At its height, the Han dynasty government held great power, but by the second century it was faltering, approaching its fall. Ministers and royal relatives manipulated the power of the central government; local garrisons fought battles with each other; floods and droughts were ceaseless, farmlands became deserted, and famine omnipresent; chaos spread throughout the land. According to the historical records, in the year 153, about one third of the counties in the country were stricken by floods or locust plagues. Tens of thousands of peasant families fell into destitution, becoming homeless and hopeless. Much of the country was engaged in bitter conflict, and peasant rebellions were common. There were more than one hundred uprisings reported in historical records during the reigns of Emperor An and Emperor Ling (107–188 CE).

In such times of chaos, people yearned for Laozi's ideal government based on "order through non-action" to become once again a
reality. They also dreamed they could escape from their own personal plights and live their lives as immortals; thus the already pre-
vailing doctrines of immortals and Huang-Lao Daoism were even
more welcomed. Meanwhile, increasing numbers of occult practitioners (*fangshi*) appeared, claiming to be able to tell of people's for-
tunes, futures, and deaths, to command ghosts and deities, and to
predict and explain social change through astrology. Also during
this time, various versions of the *Book of Supreme Peace* (*Taiping
Jing*) circulated among the masses, promising a forthcoming new
era of supreme peace and prosperity.

According to Han dynasty histories, the earliest incarnation of
the *Book of Supreme Peace* was actually made up of two related
works, *The Celestial Calendar* and the *Book of the Initiation of the Era
of Supreme Peace,* and was compiled by Gan Zhongke from the state
of Qi during Emperor Cheng's reign (32–7 BCE) through the end
of the Former Han dynasty. It predicted the collapse of the Han
dynasty, and reported that the Supreme God had already sent an
immortal named Chijingzi (Pure Energy Master) to teach the people how to establish a society of great peace to replace the dying
Han dynasty. Subsequently, the local government imprisoned Gan
for "obscuring the emperor and confusing the masses." During the
reign of Emperor Ai (7–1 BCE), the last emperor of the Former
Han dynasty, a disciple of Gan named Xia Huoliang, was sentenced
to death by the government because he had inherited and promulgated the *Book of Supreme Peace.* During the reign of Emperor Shun

(125–144 CE), the last years of the Later Han dynasty, another version of the the *Book of Supreme Peace* called the *Book of Pure Commands of the Supreme Peace* (*Taiping Qingling Shu*) appeared once again among the masses. It is recorded in the *History of the Later Han* that this work was a sacred scripture conferred to Yuji by Quyang Quan. Modern scholars speculate that the *Book of Pure Commands of the Supreme Peace* was the same book as *The Celestial Calendar* and the *Book of Initiation of the Era of Supreme Peace;* the differences, mostly of supplementary material, came

STATUE OF THE FIRST CELESTIAL MASTER.

from clandestine transcriptions circulating among the common folk for decades. These two books, the full texts of which are unfortunately lost, appear only as an abstract in the *Daoist Canon* compiled during the Ming dynasty. The abstract of the the *Book of Supreme Peace* was edited by Luqiu Fangyuan (?–902) from Suzhou (now in Jiangsu Province) at the end of the Tang dynasty. He thought the *Taiping Qingling Shu* was overly verbose, and too inconvenient for readers. He abridged the original seventeen scrolls of each section into one scroll, reducing the original one hundred and seventy scrolls to ten. Fortunately, he gives us a glimpse into the nature of the original; otherwise, we would know next to nothing of the work. From this abstract of the *Taiping Qingling Shu,* we can note the following points:

First, the text adopted the cosmology expressed in the *Daode Jing:* "Dao generates one. One generates two. Two generates three. Three generates the ten thousand natural things." Dao is the origin of the universe as well as its controller, its driving force, and its end.

Second, the text taught the unity of Heaven and Man, as well as correspondences between them. It explained in detail that all that transpired in the human world, including birth, aging, illness and death, prosperity versus adversity, blessing versus curses, were correlated with or determined by changes of the celestial bodies.

Third, it preached that people could live forever, without death; they could become immortals by cultivating Dao. It further offered a set of cultivation methods, the longest and most detailed of the contents of the *Book of Supreme Peace.* Humans are divided into seven groups: godlike people, true people, immortal people, sagely people, virtuous people, common people and slave people. The first three groups can live forever without death. People can elevate themselves to higher levels as long as they continue cultivating Dao. Concerning the cultivation methods, the book suggests that the life of human beings comes from the harmonious co-existence of *shen* (spirit) and *qi* (energy). The way to live long is to "store *qi*" and "unite *shen*"; one should use *shen* to accumulate *qi*, and the let *jing* (essence), *qi,* and *shen* merge into one. This method of cultivation is called "concentration on one."

Finally, the text declares political equality among all people, and elaborately criticizes the social and economic injustice of the times. It likens those who are "rich but cruel" to rats in granaries, accusing them of monopolizing wealth and disregarding the lives of others. This situation was caused, it claims, by the loss of Dao. It proposes that the rule of Dao would take the people as the foundation; the emperor and ministers could not keep the country in order without the support of common people; the emperor and ministers should work hard day and night, and concern themselves with people's sufferings. In a dialogue claimed to have taken place between the Supreme Deity and the text's author, a plan was established for a millennium of "Three Qi Harmony," meaning harmony among Heaven, Earth, and Humanity, harmony among emperor, minister and people, as well as harmony among father, mother, and son.

This kind of ideology would lead to bloody insurrections among the peasantry a few decades later, during which the earliest Daoist orders were organized. The most formidable rebellions were those of the Five Bushels Sect founded by Zhang Daoling and the Supreme Peace Sect created by the Three Zhangs. The central text of these early Daoist orders, along with the *Daode Jing*, was the *Taiping Jing*.

Zhang Daoling, otherwise known as Zhangling, was born in the state of Pei (now part of Jiangsu Province) around the year 34 CE. He once was a local official in Jiangzhou County, Baling Prefecture (now in Chongqing Municipality). However, he soon resigned to cultivate the arts of immortality. Historical records describe him as an avid believer in Huang-Lao Daoism, and that he retreated into Mount Heming to cultivate these beliefs. He claimed to have composed a book of twenty-four chapters under dictation from "the Supreme Master Lao" (Laozi) and began his missionary work in 141 CE. He elevated the *Daode Jing* to canonical status, deified Laozi as Lord of Daoism, labeled his followers as "spiritual soldiers," ordained himself as leader, established the twenty-four districts of his followers, and sent sacrificial masters to organize them.

Zhang's major activity was the treatment of patients with magical water (*fushui*, with *fu* being a paper charm, *shui* meaning water) and penance rituals (*huiguo*). *Fushui* also describes the technique by which the practitioner empowered a piece of paper using charmed seals or a bowl of water by chanting spells. After burning the charmed paper in a bowl and mixing the ashes with water, the patient would drink the solution. Another technique was *huiguo,* in which a patient seeking healing was asked to write out all his or her sins and failures, after which the writing was burned. Sometimes the patient would just confess silently in meditation before the gods. Zhang instituted a standard tithe of five bushels of rice for these treatments. In large part due to this system, the Five Bushels Sect spread rapidly in Sichuan and southern Shaanxi.

Zhang Daoling adapted the early explanation of the *Daode Jing* from Xiang'er's *Commentary on Laozi* to serve his religious goals. It is speculated that Xiang'er is the honorific of Zhang Daoling or perhaps his grandson Zhanglu. From the remnant scrolls of this commentary discovered in the Mogao Caves in Dunhuang, we can see is that it quoted a good deal from the *Book of Supreme Peace,* and has a close relationship to that work in general. Zhang Daoling writes in this book that "the One" disperses to become *qi*, while *qi* coalesces to become the Supreme Master Lao. One is Dao. He personified the philosophical Dao as the celestial god Supreme Master Lao. Furthermore, Zhang advises believers to perform more benefactions; longevity is the reward for virtues, death is the punishment for crimes; people can live forever if they abide by the commandments and perform good deeds.

When Zhang Daoling died in the year 156, one of his sons, Zhangheng, succeeded to his father's position. When Zhangheng passed away in 179, Zhanglu, his son, took the post. According to historical records, the Five Bushels Sect further expanded

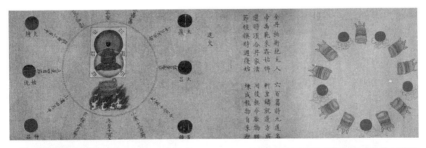

TWO SECTIONS OF A SONG DYNASTY SCROLL ILLUSTRATING THE PROCESS OF COMPOUNDING ELIXIRS.

Zhanglu's rule. He defeated several local powers in southern Shaanxi, gaining control of those regions along with Sichuan. There he established a regional theocracy of the Five Bushels Sect, and titled himself as "Teacher Ruler." His government offered free lodgings along with grain and meat to poor travelers, forbade the slaughter of animals during the first half of the year (considered the period of gestation and rearing of young), restricted the production of alcohol, and established a lenient system of justice. Punishment for slight violations of the sectarian prescripts was to build roads as compensation; sentences were imposed only upon those who had offended three times or more. This governance lasted over thirty years, and reportedly was heartily welcomed by the people, who lived and labored in peace and contentment.

When Caocao (a prime minister who during the collapse of the Han actually became more powerful than the emperor) raised troops against his mini-state in 215, Zhanglu surrendered and was enfoeffed as Duke Langzhong, then was appointed as General Zhennan (literally, "Guard the South"). The Five Bushels Sect was able to survive and Zhang Daoling was eventually honored as "Celestial Master," with Zhanglu accorded the title "Heir Master."

The three brothers Zhangjiao, Zhangbao, and Zhangliang were born in Julu, Hebei. They also were advocates of Huang-Lao Daoism, who preached the precepts of the *Daode Jing* among the masses and also secretly spread the program of the Supreme Peace sect. Their methods were similar to those of the Five Bushels Sect, also employing *fushui* techniques. After more than ten years, they had hundreds of thousands of followers scattered throughout the

eastern prefectures of You, Ji, Qing, Xu, Yang, and Yu. These masses erupted in a great rebellion in the year 184; since their followers wrapped yellow bands of cloth around their heads, the rebellion has come to be known as the Yellow Turban Rebellion. It was
the greatest uprising since the rebellion of Chensheng and
Wuguang at the end of the Qin dynasty. Regional warlords across
the country banded together and eventually crushed the uprising,
and the three Zhang brothers were killed. The Supreme Peace Sect
was forbidden and, in fact, many of its followers converted to the
Five Bushels Sect.

Besides the three generations of Zhang Daoling and the three
Zhang brothers, there was another founder of a Daoist organization
of note, the remarkable Zhangxiu. Originally a follower of Zhang
Daoling, he later established his own religious sect in southern
Shaanxi, the rituals of which were quite similar those the Five
Bushels Sect. His group rose up to echo the revolt of the Supreme
Peace Sect, and eventually merged with that of Zhanglu.

The establishment of the Five Bushels and Supreme Peace sects
prove that the earliest founders of Daoist sects took the *Taiping Jing*
as their common text and preached Huang-Lao Daoism to the
masses in a turbulent era. They helped poor farmers with healing
charms and by curing illnesses. Having gained the allegiance of a
large number of farmers, they organized these followers into Daoist
groups. Thus in the earliest Daoist organizations, poor farmers
composed the main membership, and their ideology advocated
resistance to the cruelty imposed by the ruling class. These smaller
groups soon merged into the Five Bushels Sect.

THE LINEAGE OF CELESTIAL MASTERS

Because Zhang Daoling was honored as Celestial Master after the Jin dynasty (third century CE), the Five Bushels Sect eventually became known as the Celestial Master Sect. Celestial Master also became the hereditary title for Zhang's successors. From the Tang dynasty (618–907)) to modern times, this title has been the symbol of the highest authority in the Zhengyi Sect (further explained in Chapter 3), and has throughout history been recognized by emperors as well. In the history of feudal China, only two family lines have been so unanimously honored from dynasty to dynasty, no matter the chaos of war or changes of regime. One is that of the Confucian sages of Qufu, Shandong, and the other is that of the Celestial Masters of Mount Dragon and Tiger, Jiangxi.

According to the *Annals of Mount Dragon and Tiger*, the succession of the Celestial Masters was strictly stipulated: the Celestial Mastership "may not be transferred to a brother if any son exists; may not be transferred to a grandson if any brother exists; may not be transferred to a brother-in-law if any grandson exists; may not be transferred to a nephew if any brother-in-law exists; may not be transferred to an uncle if any nephew exists; may not be transferred to any other family member if any uncle exists; may not be transferred to a non-family member if any family member exists." The lineage holds three sacred ceremonial objects: the book of twenty-four scrolls bequeathed by Laozi, the charm seal of Governor Yangping, and the sword for slaying demons also given by Supreme Master Lao. There had been thirty-six generations in this lineage prior to 1949, called "The Lineage of the Celestial Master of the Han

CELESTIAL MASTERS MANSION, THE FOUNDER TEMPLE OF THE ZHENGYI DENOMINATION AT MOUNT DRAGON AND TIGER. JIANGXI PROVINCE.

Dynasty." This lineage was broken in 1969 when the last heir passed away in Taipei, Taiwan, leaving no offspring.

It is interesting to note that while the birthplace of Confucius was Qufu, in Shandong Province, and the lineage of Confucian sages always hailed from that town, Zhang Daoling's hometown is *not* Guixi in Jiangxi Province. According to the Daoist scripture called the *Lineage of Celestial Masters in the Han Dynasty,* in the years of Emperor He's reign (88–105), Zhang visited all of the famous sacred places for cultivation, until finally he, along with his disciple, Zhaochang, came to Mount Yunjin (Brocade Cloud Mountain) in Guixi County, guided by two fairy cranes. Attracted by the elegant scenery and its wise and powerful residents, he stopped to concoct some elixirs. After three years of hard effort, he was rewarded with efficacious results, and a dragon and a tiger appeared before him. From then on, this mountain was renamed as Mount Dragon and Tiger. It is from this mountain that Zhang Daoling started out on his missionary journey, which eventually led to the founding of religious Daoism. After his surrender to Caocao, Zhanglu and some of his followers were dispersed to the areas around Luoyang and Yecheng in Henan. When Zhangsheng, son of Zhanglu, took over the sect, Caocao offered him grain (a kind of currency at that time) and protection, but Zhangsheng declined the offer, and returned, with the sword and seal passed down from Zhang Daoling, to Guixi, where the Lineage of Celestial Masters has settled ever since.

Since Guixi in Jiangxi Province thus came to be considered the birthplace of Daoism, many Daoist relics have been preserved there. Among them, the most important attractions are True Unity Temple and Supreme Pure Temple on Mount Dragon and Tiger, as well as the Celestial Master Mansion at the foot of the mountain. Zhengyi Temple was built at the place where Zhang Daoling made his elixirs, but the earliest date of its construction remains unknown. Throughout history it has been a place for disciples to offer sacrifices to Zhang Daoling. Daoist priests come to worship him, offering many hymns dedicated to their spiritual leader. The formal monastic buildings were built around the tenth century. According to the existing stele in front of Celestial Master Temple on Mount Dragon and Tiger, construction on the temple began in the Baoda era of the Southern Tang dynasty in the Five Dynasties and Ten Kingdoms period (907–979); during the Song dynasty (960–1279), it underwent several expansions and restorations.

Having been further enlarged during the Ming dynasty (1368–1644), it received its present name, True Unity Temple. During the Qing dynasty (1644–1911), this temple was a compound of three hall buildings, occupying 20 hectares. It was planned that the offspring of Celestial Master Zhang would live here to burn incense and worship. Unfortunately, it was destroyed by a fire in the 1940s, leaving only the foundation.

Supreme Pure Temple, about eight kilometers from Supreme Pure Village, is the place where past generations of Celestial Masters held ceremonies. It is said that there once was a thatched cottage wherein Zhang Daoling performed exorcisms; therefore, according to Daoist teachings, it is also the place where deities and ghosts accepted the appointments of new Celestial Masters. Zhangsheng originally set up an altar in this temple for conferring his charms and ordaining his disciples. Since then there have been annual assemblies for charm delivery and priesthood ordination on specified days. Fires and floods damaged these buildings, and they were restored and even expanded countless times during the Song, Yuan, Ming, and Qing dynasties. The temple was formally renamed Supreme True Unity Temple in 1114, in the third year of the reign of Emperor Huizong of the Song dynasty.

Celestial Master Mansion has been the living compound of the Celestial Masters from generation to generation. It is in Supreme Pure Town at the foot of Mount Dragon and Tiger, and is one of several existing residence palaces in China bearing the title of "The First Home in Southern China." It is said that construction began in the twelfth century, during the Song dynasty. Having undergone a good deal of reconstruction, the existing buildings, of which major portions remain from the Qing dynasty, include a gate, central hall, meditation hall, ceremonial hall, library, and garden. The structures take various styles of storied houses, platforms, large halls, and penthouses; the pillars, girders, walls, and roofs are decorated with frescos and sculptures; the old, sky-high trees shade the yards like woods; a brook flows alongside the gate, where there is a vertical tablet on which is inscribed the characters: "Mansion of Heirs to Celestial Master of Han Dynasty." The central hall is the official place of the Celestial Masters; the meditation hall is the living compound of the Celestial Masters' families, with main, front rooms, wing rooms, and corridors; the ceremonial hall is the sacrificial shrine of the Celestial Masters and their families, where the statues of major Daoist deities as well as Zhang Daoling were enshrined. It is said that the sword and seal kept in the Mansion are those passed down from Zhang Daoling.

CHAPTER 3

THE DEVELOPMENT OF DAOISM AND THE FORMING OF SECTS

FROM THE CELESTIAL MASTERS TO ZHENGYI DAO

Over the nearly two thousand years of the development of the religion of Daoism many denominations and sects have come into being due to differences in interpretations of teachings, lineages, and transmission, and methods of organizing and forming institutions. There are eighty-six denominations and sects recorded in documents at White Cloud Temple in Beijing. After the 15th century, more eclectic sects emerged among the people because of Daoist intercourse with Confucianism and Buddhism. Among these numerous sects, some were named after famous historical masters, some after their places of origin, some after particular Daoist scriptures they followed, and some after cultivation methods. However, throughout history there have been only four widely recognized major denominations, which can be categorized in turn under one of the two systems of Zhengyi Dao (Orthodox Unity Dao) and Quanzhen Dao (Complete Realization Dao).

Zhengyi Dao evolved directly from the Celestial Masters Way. In the middle of the 3rd century, central China was reunited after many decades of war and chaos. The Celestial Masters Way began to develop in two directions: on one hand, it continued to spread widely among poor farmers, continuing to emerge in the doctrines of organizations fighting against the oppression of the ruling class. Among the numerous insurrections conducted in the name of Daoism, one lead by Sun'en and Luxun during the 3rd century was the largest and most devastating. After these rebellions were thoroughly crushed, Daoism lost much of its original attraction to and influence over farmers. On the other hand, many nobles began to follow the Celestial Masters Way. The world of immortals proposed by Daoism, rather than notions of an equal society, sparked the interest of many in the upper classes. Intellectuals were attracted to Daoism, adapting its doctrines to their personal spiritual pursuits;

THE AZURE CLOUD TEMPLE OF MOUNT TAI. SHANDONG PROVINCE.

thus many wrote new treatises on Daoist tenets and many Daoist ceremonies and ritual practices were accordingly adjusted. Thus, during this period of fragmentation of China following the four centuries of the Han, a Daoist reformation took place, with thinkers like Gehong (284–364), of the Eastern Jin dynasty, Kou Qianzhi (365–448), of the Northern Wei dynasty, Lu Xiujing (406–477), of the Liu Song dynasty, and Tao Hongjin (456–536), of the Liang dynasty leading the way.

The inner and outer chapters of *Baopuzi* (*The Philosopher Who Embraces Simplicity*) by Gehong were canonized by later Daoists as major theoretical works. Gehong shifted the goal of Daoist ideology from a pursuit of millennial salvation to one of personal delivery and immortality. He argued eloquently for the existence of immortals and the possibility of immortality through self-cultivation, and meticulously itemized various methods of cultivation and alchemy. He also re-annotated Daoist theological works according to Confucian thought, argued Daoist cultivation practice was consistent with Confucian morality, and accepted Confucian norms of righteous words and deeds as being a necessary precondition of cultivation. Thus nobles and intellectuals welcomed his work.

Kou Qianzhi lived in the years of the split between the Southern and Northern dynasties. Supported by imperial family members and nobles of the Northern dynasty, he claimed to have been visited by Supreme Master Lao, who gave him the title of Celestial Master, along with the *New Musical Liturgy of Commandments from the Clouds* (clouds representing the heavenly realm), a classic in 20 scrolls. He courageously reformed the teachings of the Celestial Masters Way

A CHANTING CEREMONY TAKING PLACE IN THE LAOLU HALL OF WHITE CLOUD TEMPLE, BEIJING.

during the Northern dynasty, rectified its organizations, instituted liturgical and musical rules, compiled scriptures, and subsequently established the New Celestial Masters Way, also often referred to as the Northern Celestial Masters Way, in the capital city of Pingcheng (now Datong in Shanxi Province) during the Northern Wei dynasty. Kou successfully effected the unification of Daoism with feudal power.

Lu Xiujing lived in southern China. His major contribution was to inherit and develop Gehong's theories and apply them in the reformation of extant Daoist organizations. He collected large numbers of Daoist scriptures and improved liturgies. His reformed Daoism is called the Southern Celestial Masters Way.

Tao Hongjing also inherited Gehong's theories. He enriched and developed Daoist cosmology on the basis of Laozi and the *Yijing* (*Book of Changes*). He was among the earliest advocates for the unification of Confucianism, Buddhism, and Daoism. In his *Catalogue of the Daoist Pantheon,* he arranged various Daoist deities into a great hierarchical system for the first time, and promoted the unification and systematization of Daoist theories.

In 364, during the Eastern Jin dynasty, a Daoist priest named Yangxi claimed that the goddess Madam Wei had given him a scripture in 31 scrolls titled the *True Book of Shangqing* (*shangqing* means "supreme purity"). He subsequently founded the Shangqing Sect, which took the *True Book of Shangqing* as its central text, promoted the Heavenly King of the Origin and Supreme Master Lao as its two highest celestial gods, and adopted a practice called *cunxiang* as its chief method of cultivation. By this method, a practitioner can guide celestial gods into his body and communicate with the gods of his own internal organs. The practitioner's internal gods report his or her behavior to the celestial gods, who in turn raise or lower the practitioner's status. Followers continue with this practice until they are ready to ascend to heaven as

THE HIGHEST SKY PALACE. MOUNT MAO, JIANGSU PROVINCE.

immortals. As this practice became more widespread, the sect became popular on Mount Mao, in Jiangsu Province.

There are some Daoists who have chosen the *Sacred Jewel Scriptures* as their central texts. This tradition is the called Lingbao Sect (*lingbao* translates roughly as "sacred jewel"). Its main characteristics include declaring universal salvation, paying special attention to liturgies and rituals, and emphasizing moral conversions. Its most sacred mountain is Mount Gezao in Jiangxi Province.

Many other Daoist sects, including the Pure Bright (Jingming) Sect, the Highest Heaven (Shenxiao) Sect, the Dragon Tiger (Longhu) Sect, the Wudang Sect (which originated at Mount

Wudang), and the Pure Beauty (Qingwei) Sect, continued to emerge throughout the Jin, Tang, and Song dynasties. They both coexisted and communicated, learning from each other.

This changed in 1304, during Yuan Dynasty, when the emperor granted the honorific title of Orthodoxy Oneness Lord (Zhengyi Lord) to Zhang Yucai, the 38th generation Celestial Master, and placed him in charge of all Daoist sects in China. Since then, Southern and Northern Celestial Master Sects, the Shangqing Sect, and the Lingbao Sect, have been generally called Zhengyi Dao. Their common characteristics are: they take Zhengyi classics as their central scriptures; they undertake liturgy and exorcist rituals as their major religious services; their clerics are allowed to marry and have children; they are not forced to live in temples and lead monastic lives; and their commandments are not particularly strict. Zhengyi Dao is the general name for all kinds of talismanic sects directed from Mount Dragon and Tiger, formed after Daoism had already entered a relatively mature stage. Among the sects in this denomination, some have preserved their own unique tenets and liturgies, whilst others have conformed to Zhengyi norms.

THE ESTABLISHMENT AND TRAITS OF QUANZHEN DAO

It used to be claimed that the Quanzhen denomination of Daoism had a very long history, originating from the celestial god called Royal Lord of the East, and descending from Zhong Lihan and Lu Dongbin (both ancient Chinese ancestor-heroes). In fact, its origin was significantly later: it was established by a Daoist named Wang Chongyang around the 12th century. Wang Chongyang was born in Xianyang, Shaanxi Province, in 1113. It was a time of migration and reconfiguration of ethnic populations and cultures in North China. The Northern Song dynasty (960–1127) was quickly replaced by the Jin dynasty (1115–1234), established by the Nuzhen minority from northern Asia. Daoism, as an ancient component of indigenous Chinese culture, was confronted with foreign culture and religious thought; the complicated ethnic and social contradictions demanded new doctrines and new canons. Hence a new denomination arose quite different from Zhengyi Dao.

Wang Chongyang claimed that in 1159, at a place called Gahe, he had encountered the immortal Lu Dongbin, who offered him divine drink and taught him Daoist truth. Wang immediately left his family for Mount Zhongnan to cultivate Dao. In 1167 he left the mountain and moved eastward, arrived at the coast at Shandong, and began his missionary work of organizing an order. He recognized his foremost seven disciples—Mayu, Sun Bu'er, Tan Chuduan, Liu Chuxuan, Qiu Chuji, Wang Chuyi and Hao Datong—and established the earliest Quanzhen groups in Wendeng, Ninghai, Fushan, Dengzhou, and Laizhou, all in Shandong Province. Five orders were originally established: the

Three Religions Seven Jewels Society, Three Religions Golden Lotuses Society, Three Religions Three Constellations Society, Three Religions Jade Flowers Society, and Three Religions Equality Society. "Three religions" refers to the ultimate unity of Daoism, Confucianism, and Buddhism. The influence of these societies was great and followers gathered quickly.

Wang Chongyang incorporated poetic ballads into his sermons to make his ideas more understandable to and acceptable by the masses. The collections of his writings and poems compiled by his disciples include: the *Collection of Chongyang on Perfect Realization* (twelve scrolls); *Collection of Chongyang's Instructions* (three scrolls); *Chongyang's Fifteen Treatises on the Establishment of Daoism*; and

DOUBLE YANG PALACE. HU COUNTY, SHAANXI PROVINCE.

Chongyang's Twenty-Four Oral Teachings for Danyang. Wang Chongyang established a set of innovative religious theories and practices by developing and refining the original Daoist doctrines of salvation, contentment in poverty, and abstinence. He deemed Daoism to be identical with Buddhism and Confucianism in nature and origin, all of which are true but different in name. He summarized the tenets of his Neo-Daoism as "the unification of the three religions," and taught that only through such unification can the right path be found. Quanzhen is variously translated as "all true," or "complete truth," or "complete realization," but a more precise meaning of the term derives from the expanded expression *du quan qi zhen,* which means that a follower should, through detachment from worldly temptations, preserve his or her true nature. Here we will use the Chinese Quanzhen to refer to this school because all these terms lose something in translation. We should note of this belief system that:

First, Wang requested his converts to study not only Daoist scriptures such as the *Daode Jing* and the *Book of Pure Silence,* but also the *Heart Sutra* of Buddhism and the *Classic of Filial Piety* of Confucianism. He deemed Daoism, Buddhism, and Confucianism to be interpretations of the same truth, like three branches of the same tree.

Second, Wang combined commandments and teachings of Daoism, Confucianism, and Buddhism to establish the fundamental principles of the Quanzhen Dao. In *Chongyang's Fifteen Treatises on the Establishment of Daoism,* Wang prescribed the general rules of cultivation requirements and behavioral standards in fifteen issues:

1) *monastic life,* which demands all Quanzhen monks to live collectively in monasteries; 2) *spiritual wanderings,* which demands that Quanzhen Daoists often visit other mountains and temples to pay homage and learn from each other; 3) *literary study,* which demands that Daoists read classical works, not necessarily in great number but in great depth; 4) *medicinal study,* which demands that Daoists master medicine, otherwise it is impossible to understand the Dao; 5) *shelter of Dao,* which requests that Daoists live in huts instead of large buildings (a precept forgotten by his disciples soon after his death, when the denomination flourished under the support of emperors and nobles, allowing many monks to live in palatial monasteries); 6) *partnership,* which demands that Daoists choose virtuous, wise, and aspiring partners for cultivation; 7) *meditation,* which demands that the mind of a person in meditation be as quiet and stable as Mount Tai, free from any worldly concerns; 8) *mind taming,* which demands that those who meditate eliminate distracting ideas; 9) *refining original character,* which demands Daoists have a gentle temperament; 10) *five-element matching,* by which the cultivator guides the *qi* of the five internal organs into harmonious intercourse; 11) *blending of xing and ming,* which is to make *xing* (original nature) and *ming* (vital energy) rely on and promote each other; 12) a *sacred way,* which guides followers to cultivate themselves through harsh conditions over many years and to accumulate the power to elevate to Heaven; 13) *transcendence from Three Realms,* which is to transcend the realms of desire, the material world, and finally, the void; 14) *True Body cultivation,* which is the cultivation of the body's original nature; 15)

STATUE OF MASTER QIU CHUJI (CENTER), FOUNDER OF THE WHITE CLOUD TEMPLE IN BEIJING. STYLED CHANGCHUNZI (ETERNAL SPRING MASTER), QIU WAS A DISCIPLE OF MASTER WANG CHONGYANG, AND FOUNDED THE DRAGON GATE SECT OF QUANZHEN DAOISM. HE TRAVELED TO CENTRAL ASIA AND WON THE SUPPORT OF GENGHIS KHAN FOR HIS RELIGIOUS ACTIVITIES.

breaking from the mundane, which means not to physically leave the mundane world in pursuit of longevity, but to leave it mentally whilst one's body continues to inhabit it.

Thirdly, Wang synthesized Daoist theories of inner alchemy with Zen Buddhist concepts, denied the importance of theories and words, and concentrated on cultivation practices. He assumed that what is fundamental to cultivating and realizing Dao is a person's unchangeable and genuine nature. He advocated reaching the pure and quiet realm by "understanding one's mind and discovering one's original nature."

Fourthly, Wang Chongyang established an overall system of communal religious life for his Quanzhen order, borrowing greatly from Buddhism.

In 1170, Wang Chongyang died in Kaifeng, Henan Province. His disciples Mayu and Tan Chuduan took over the management of the Quanzhen denomination. The seven top disciples founded sects of their own: Mayu, honored as Danyangzi (Yang Elixir Master), set up the Immortal Encounter Sect; Tan Chuduan, honored as Changzhenzi (Eternal Perfect Master), founded the Southern Emptiness Sect; Hao Datong, honored as Guangningzi (Broad Peace Master), founded the Mount Hua Sect; Wang Chuyi, honored as Yuyangzi (Jade Yang Master), founded the Mount Yu Sect; Liu Chuxuan, honored as Changshengzi (Master of Long Life), established the Mount Sui Sect; Sun Bu'er, wife of Mayu, set up the Pure Silence Sect (as a female disciple, her works which dealt with cultivation methods for women are the major guides for female practitioners); Qiu Chuji, honored as Changchunzi (Eternal

Spring Master), established the Dragon Gate Sect. With recognition and support from Genghis Khan, the Dragon Gate Sect (Longmen Pai) eventually became the most influential group, with which most Quanzhen temples in mainland China, Hong Kong, Macao, Taiwan, and Southeast Asia are today affiliated. The current headquarters of the China Taoist Association is located in White Cloud Temple in Beijing, which is honored as the founding temple of the Dragon Gate Sect.

While Wang Chongyang was establishing Quanzhen Dao in northern China, the Southern School of Alchemy, which also claimed to trace its history back to Zhong Liquan and Lu Dongbin,

DAOIST CEREMONIAL ROBE AND HUAYUAN HAT WITH LOTUS TOP.

was spreading in southern China under the rule of the Southern Song dynasty. Their methods were to make inner elixirs by refining and concentrating essence, energy, and spirit through the three processes of physical cultivation, energy cultivation, and spiritual cultivation. Li Daochun, the founder of this group, borrowed from Confucianism and Buddhism and worked them into a Daoist framework. He believed that the ideals of cultivation in all three ideologies were essentially identical in that they could not exist without "central harmony" and thus affirmed the inner alchemical method of "central harmony." He established his own sect, integrating some theories and methods of Chan (perhaps more familiar by the name of its Japanese variant, Zen) including studies of *koan* (the Japanese word for the seemingly insoluble puzzles that a practitioner is assigned to meditate upon) and the striking of meditators with a stick to promote sudden enlightenment.

After the collapse of the Southern Song dynasty in 1279, Quanzhen groups spread into southern China, and Li Daochun claimed that the Southern School of Alchemy originally belonged to the Quanzhen denomination. Li Daochun along with the four masters prior to him are honored as the Five Southern Masters.

As for clothing style, in their daily lives, Quanzhen monks wear dark colored robes, and grow long hair that is kept in a wispy bun, topped with a Daoist cap. Monks and nuns dress in the same style. Daoists have especially prescribed costumes for ceremonies, in which the major players in the rituals have embroidered, colored robes. Zhengyi Dao priests wear clothing similar wear to that of Quanzhen monks in ceremonies and rituals, while their daily dress is quite plain, little different from that of ordinary people. They also are not required to grow their hair long and can shave. Zhengyi Daoist priests are not forced to keep a vegetarian diet, though they may not eat dog meat or beef, because they believe dogs are a symbol of fidelity and oxen and bulls are a farmer's helpers.

There were once other important Daoist sects in China, among which the most famous were Taiyi (Great Unity) Daoism, and Zhenda (True Great) Daoism. However, they have since disappeared; only the Zhengyi Dao and Quanzhen Dao denominations have survived.

CHAPTER 4

DAOIST DEITIES

WHAT OR WHO ARE DAOIST DEITIES?

Deities, also called immortals, are the basic objects of Daoist faith. They are the personification of Dao, which is the origin and essence of the universe, as well as the ultimate goal pursued by Daoists. According to Daoism, deities are somewhat similar to human beings in appearance, so they are variously called sacred persons, immortal persons, supreme persons, and perfected persons, and are like those who have realized truth, or obtained enlightenment. Still, they are quite different from ordinary people.

First of all, deities possess the essence of the origin of the universe, or original *qi*, because they either arose from the origination of the universe and are thus incarnations of original *qi*, or they have returned to such a state through cultivation. Secondly, deities are immortals; they do not die, because their lives are identical with Dao. They are the role models of Daoists, and also are the role models of common people, inspiring them to cultivate themselves in pursuit of reaching the highest realm of "long life without death." Thirdly, deities have powers surpassing those of ordinary mortals, enabling such pursuits as speeding across the sky, controlling the course of wind and rain, and determining blessings and

THE EIGHT IMMORTALS OF DAOISM.

misfortunes. They can dominate or control all earthly phenomenon, and people must obey their will or they will incur punishment. Fourthly, the celestial world they live in is similar to the mundane world in that it has a strict hierarchical order and effective management. Every deity must act in accordance with his or her own position and duties, and obey his or her superiors. Fifthly, deities have clear division of labor in terms of overseeing the mundane world. They have missions to convert people, undertake poetic justice, perform benefactions and exorcisms, and so on. Therefore Daoists not only see immortals as ideal role models, but also as protectors of humanity.

Most Daoist deities live in Heaven, but some inhabit the mundane world. The places dominated by deities are called Sacred Abodes and Blessed Lands. There are ten Major Sacred Skies and thirty-six Minor Skies, where all affairs are managed by immortals sent from Heaven; and seventy-two Blessed Lands where perfect

PORTRAIT OF THE PURE JADE EMPEROR, HUNG OVER THE ALTER DURING TEMPLE FESTIVITIES.

persons from Heaven, whose celestial ranks are inferior to immortals, manage all other affairs. These places are believed to be perfect places of cultivation, where many famous Daoists of the past have dwelt, cultivated Dao, and achieved immortality. These are the sacred places of Daoism, and Daoist temples and relics are usually found there.

There are many deities in Daoism, and for the newcomer, clearly differentiating all the deities and their tasks is a bit overwhelming. Hopefully this chapter will at least give the reader a sense of the scope of the Daoist pantheon and the characteristics of some of its deities. Immortal persons and perfected persons are two titles for deities with different ranks. Throughout history, there were various statements concerning the deities' hierarchy. The *Book of Supreme Peace* divided deities into six categories, while Gehong's *The Philosopher Who Embraces Simplicity* divided them into three categories, and *Supreme Perfect Liturgies* into nine. Here we approximately group them into celestial gods, constellation gods, territorial gods, and vagabond gods.

AN INTRODUCTION TO DAOIST DEITIES

The supreme gods in Daoism are the Three Pure Ones: "The Pure Jade Heavenly Sage of the Yuanshi (before the origin of the universe)," "The Heavenly Sage of the Supreme Pure Lingbao (sacred jewel)," and "The Heavenly Sage of Dao and its Virtues in the Realm Shangqing (supreme purity)." In Daoist history it was only after the 9th century that Daoists worshiped the Three Pure Ones as the highest celestial gods. In early Daoism, The Sovereign Pure Realm, Supreme Pure Realm, and Great Pure Realm were simply the three highest celestial realms inhabited by many celestial gods, rather than ruled by any particular ones. During Tang Emperor Wuzong's reign (841–846), the "Heavenly Sage of the Primordial Origin," "The Great Master of Supreme Dao," and "The Great Master of Supreme Lao," were deified as the highest celestial gods, while "The Heavenly Precious Master of the Sovereign Pure Realm," the "Sacred Precious Master of the Supreme Pure Realm," and the "Holy Precious Master of the Great Pure Realm," were called the "Three Precious Masters," and considered the second highest rank of celestial gods. After the 12th century, the highest celestial deities and the Three Precious Masters were gradually incorporated into one set of three deities, while the secondary Three Pure Gods were transformed into the Three Pure Realms where the three highest gods dwelled.

The Heavenly Sage of the Origin, more commonly called the Pure Jade Emperor, is the highest of the Three Pure Ones, living in the Sovereign Pure Realm. He is the creator of the universe, and was born before its origin. He is composed of primordial *qi*, and is eternal and imperishable. He applied Dao when constructing the universe, and symbolizes Dao. His statue is usually placed on the middle altar in the temple hall of Three Pure Ones, typically appearing in the form of an old man with a shining circle behind his head and a colorful robe on his body. He either holds a red elixir pill in one hand, or his left hand shows the motion of picking something up (though still empty), while his right hand is also empty. This symbolizes the first stage of Daoist cosmology, when existence was chaotic, shapeless, and voidlike. The Winter Solstice is the festival honoring his birth.

The Heavenly Sage of the Lingbao, also called the Supreme Master of Dao or the Supreme Great Emperor, lives in the Supreme Realm, and is the second ranking of the Three Pure Ones. He was born one beautiful morning of the congealed vital energy from an auspicious cloud that impregnated his mythical mother, Madam Hong. After a gestation period of 3700 years, he was born as a human and also an embodiment of Dao. His statue is usually placed on the left altar in the halls of Three Pure Ones, also taking the form of an old man. With a *taiji* (literally "great ultimate," the symbol of the *yin-yang* duality) or *ruyi* (an S-shaped scepter believed capable of granting wishes) in his hands, his pose symbolizes the second stage of Daoist cosmological formulation, when chaos abated to become clear, and *yin* and *yang* started to separate. This was the stage of "One giving birth to two." Daoists honor his birthday on the Summer Solstice.

The Heavenly Sage of Dao and its Virtue, also called Supreme Master Lao, lives in the Supreme Pure Realm. He is believed to be

Laozi, historical founder of the Daoism during the Spring and Autumn Period. Although originally born before the universe, after his earthly mother swallowed the pure energy of the sun, she became pregnant with his reincarnated form. After a gestation period of eighty-one years he was born as a white-haired old man, and so was named Laozi, or Old Son. He was given Dao from the first two sages of the Three Pure Ones, and began to spread Dao among humans. Daoists believe the works of the Three August Ones and the Five Imperial Ones, the founding of religious Daoism by Zhang Daoling, as well as the Daoist reformation by Kou Qianzhi were all conducted under his command, and is commonly recognized as the founder of Daoism. In most iconography, he appears as a white haired and white bearded old man, with a *taiji* fan or horsetail whisk in his hands. The shrines dedicated to him are called Old Master's Hall or Supreme Pure Hall. If co-worshiped in a hall of Three Pure Ones, his statue is placed on the right altar.

The Jade Emperor is second only to the Three Pure Ones, and is the general manager of Heaven, presiding over all activities of the celestial gods. It is believed that he was originally the Celestial God or Supreme God worshiped in early China.

MING DYNASTY WOODEN STATUE OF THE PURE JADE EMPEROR, WHITE CLOUD TEMPLE, BEIJING.

Originally, he was a subordinate official of the Heavenly Sage of the Origin, but begin to acquire more importance starting in the Song dynasty (12th century) when Daoism was becoming more popular and prosperous. In the Ming and Qing dynasties, he was further elevated to be the sovereign celestial god of folk religion, so there was a saying that "While there is an Emperor on earth, there is a Jade Emperor in Heaven." Daoist scriptures record that there once was a monarch named King Pure Virtue who was married to Queen Precious Moonlight. Although they still had no children, as they grew older, they continued praying to Heaven. One night, the queen dreamed that the Supreme Master of Dao sent them a golden baby in a carriage. Soon afterwards she became pregnant and

QING DYNASTY CLAY STATUES OF THE FOUR IMPERIAL ONES, WHITE CLOUD TEMPLE, BEIJING.

gave birth to a son. However when the son grew up, he did not succeed to the throne, but instead retreated to a mountain to cultivate himself. After innumerable years of cultivation, he finally became the Jade Emperor. The image of the Jade Emperor is similar to that of an emperor of the mundane world. He has a solemn visage with a black beard, and wears a hat with a flat top with fringe hanging in the front and back. His robe is embroidered with a red dragon, and he holds a jade tablet.

The Jade Emperor is married to the Queen Mother of the West, commonly called Queen Mother. She is believed to be the essence of the Great Yin (the moon), and is in charge of all goddesses in Heaven. Any person who succeeds in realizing Dao and becoming immortal must pay a formal visit to her before making a pilgrimage to the Heavenly Sage of Pre-existence. She is also a goddess of longevity, and folk tales of her birthday party are well known to all Chinese. These stories tell of a great celebration in heaven, at which guest deities from all directions are feted and peaches of immortality are served. Anyone mortal clever enough to acquire and eat a peach from the Queen Mother's table would live forever. For this reason, Chinese often give peaches as birthday gifts.

The divine rank of the Four Imperial Ones is close to that of the Jade Emperor. However, since these four deities (three celestial kings and one celestial queen) aid the Jade Emperor, they are also called the Four Auxiliary Ones, and each has particular duties. The first is the Great Emperor of Ziwei Big Dipper. Ziwei, literally "purple beauty," is the name of the palace he dwells in, and also stands for the Big Dipper. He takes orders only from the Jade Emperor and is believed to be the incarnation of the Heavenly Sage of Pre-existence. His duties are to command all the gods of the constellations and as well the gods of mountains and rivers, and to control forces of nature such as wind, rain, and thunder. He is also the lord of natural phenomena. During the Song dynasty, he was so highly esteemed that he was often worshiped together with the Jade Emperor. In portraiture he takes the guise of emperors, wearing a flat-topped hat and dragon robes.

MING DYNASTY BRONZE STATUE OF THE GOD OF THE LITERATI, WHITE CLOUD TEMPLE, BEIJING.

The second of the Four Imperial Ones is the Great Emperor of the Gouchen Constellation, the name for the four stars on the left side of the Big Dipper (*gou* means hook, and describes the shape of the constellation). It is said that he inhabits the Gouchen Palace and presides over all constellations because of its central location. His image is also that of the emperor.

The third is the Earthly Queen of the Land Gods, abbreviated as Queen Earth. She lives in the Pistil Pearl Palace, and is responsible for the interchange of *yin* and *yang*, population growth, and beauty (especially of natural scenery). She is often grouped with the Jade Emperor, and as a pair they are called the Emperor Heaven and the Queen Earth. The image of Queen Earth is similar to that of ancient Chinese queens. She is affable and elegant, with a phoenix coronet on her head and an embroidered cape draped over her shoulders.

The fourth is the Great Emperor of Longevity of the South Pole. He is also called the Old Immortal of the South Pole or the Constellation of Longevity. Since his duties are to manage the life spans of human beings, he is quite loved and respected. He has a lumpy forehead, white hair and beard, and generally appears as a gentle and happy old man holding a gnarled cane.

There are special halls for these Four Imperial Ones in many Daoist temples. In areas where folk beliefs and traditions are popular, the Longevity Constellation is usually worshiped along with the Happiness Constellation and the Success Constellation. The Happiness Constellation is reputed to be capable of bestowing happiness and offspring on those who supplicate them in the correct manner, while the Success Constellation can bestow official rank.

There are many other deities in Daoism, among whom the most important are the following:

The Great Gods of Three Realms. Also called the Great Gods of the Three Elements, they originated from nature worship of the sky, earth, and water in early times. It was observed that nothing in the universe could live without these three basic elements, which the Three Gods personify. Annual festivals celebrating the Three Elements Gods have evolved into what are called the Triplet Days, namely: the Superior Principles Day on the fifteenth day of the first Moon, for the Heaven Element God; Medium Principles Day on the fifteenth day of the seventh Moon, for the Earth Element God; and Inferior Principles Day on the fifteenth day of the tenth Moon for the Water Element God. Daoism absorbed these existing liturgies and practices. The Five Bushels Sect used to cure followers by means of letters sent to the Three Element Gods, on which the names of patients, as well as their complaints and confessions, were written in three copies. One copy was placed on

DOUMU, THE MOTHER OF THE BIG DIPPER.

a mountain addressed to the Heaven Element God, one copy was buried in the earth addressed to the Earth Element God, and one was submerged under water for the Water Element God. People also pray to the Three Element Gods for protection. It is believed that the Heaven Element God descends to the mundane world on Superior Principles Day to bestow happiness; the Earth Element God descends on Medium Principles Day to warn against crimes; the Water Element God descends on Inferior Principles Day to exorcise evil spirits. The Three Elements Gods are commonly worshiped because of their close relationship with daily blessings and curses. There are halls for the Three Elements God in most Daoist temples, and many communities even designate special temples for the worship of these deities.

Mother of the Big Dipper. In Chinese her name is Doumu, *dou* being a large dipper, *mu* meaning mother; she is a goddess who is the mother of all stars of the Big Dipper. She is believed to have originally been Madam Ziguang (meaning "purple glow"), an imperial concubine of King Yu of the Zhou Dynasty. One spring day when strolling through her garden she suddenly felt as if she had been impregnated, and soon thereafter she gave birth to nine sons. The eldest and the second eldest sons were the emperors Gouchen and Ziwei (two of the Four Imperial Ones); the other seven sons are the seven stars of Big Dipper. The seven stars control people's times of birth including the year, month, day, and hour. It is believed that as long as people obey the orders of these gods, they will be protected from the stars and lead secure and pleasant lives.

The three eyes of Doumu's image represent heaven, earth and humanity; her four heads represent the four Lunar Mansions: the Green Dragon in the East, the White Tiger of the West, the Red Phoenix (or "Vermilion Bird") of the South, and the Black Turtle-Snake (or "Dark Warrior") of the North; her eight arms represent the eight directions. The sun and the moon on her hands symbolize heaven and earth; while the bell, the wind, the bow, the rainbow, the gold stamp, the thunder, the spear, the meteor, and the two hands with clutching fingers stand for all the stars surrounding the central Big Dipper. Doumu is also a very popular Daoist deity, and Doumu Halls can be found in most Daoist temples.

Gods of the Sexagenarian Cycle. The Sexagenarian Cycle was originally a Chinese method of measuring time. The cycle was formed by the interaction of two tables, the first called the Ten Heavenly Stems (Jia, Yi, Bing, Ding, Wu, Ji, Geng, Xin, Ren, Kui) and the Twelve Earthly Branches (Zi, Chou, Yin, Mao, Chen, Si, Wu, Wei, Shen, You, Xu, Hai). Pairing one Heavenly Stem with one Earthly Branch results in a cycle of sixty pairings (before repeating); Chinese have traditionally used them to calculate time in years. According to Daoist theology, every number or year is presided over by a particular god, called the Year God; there were therefore altogether sixty Year Gods. Year Gods protect people who are born in the year of their domain, so every person has his or her protecting god. However, if a person commits a foul act, his or her Year God will report it to the Heavenly Court, Thus whenever one's birth year arrives, one must be extremely careful in words and deeds. People often buy a red waist belt from a Daoist

MING DYNASTY BRONZE STATUE OF EMPEROR ZHENWU.

temple to stay especially mindful of their behavior, and so to have a peaceful year.

There are many versions of the names of the Sexagenarian Gods, and those recorded in Daoist scriptures are different from those on the name tablets in the Sexagenarian Hall at White Cloud Temple in Beijing. Whatever their names may be, they are almost certainly based on historical figures who performed meritorious deeds.

God of the Literati. The Chinese name Wenchang was originally the general name for the constellation of the six stars above the first star of the Big Dipper. Its common name is Wenquxing, which means literally the "Twisted Constellation of Literature." Ancient astrologers said that this constellation could confer high status upon people, so it became a popular god, thought to oversee and control exploits, fame, and rank in society. This belief was eventually absorbed into Daoism. Around the sixth century Chinese feudalistic dynasties established a system of imperial examinations to select officials; passing these exams became the most viable route to a successful official career. Sacrifice to the constellation God of the Literati consequently grew more widespread, and temples were built all over the country in honor of this deity. He was given the imperial name of Emperor of Literati, and annual celebrations were held in his honor by local governors on the third day of the second moon in the ancient Chinese calendar.

In Daoism the God of the Literati was said to be named Zhang Yazi. He was a filial son in Zitong County, Sichuan Province, during the Jin dynasty (265–420), who was deified in his hometown after he made great sacrifices on the battlefield as a commander. Around the 13th century, a Daoist author wrote a book called the *Biography of Qinghe,* using a particular method of writing in which the author channels a god, in this case the God of the Literati. This work reveals that Zhang Yazi was originally a man of the Zhou dynasty (10th century BCE), and that the Zhang Yazi born in Sichuan was actually the 73rd incarnation of this individual. The Jade Emperor assigned him the duty of presiding over the Cabinet of Literati, which is specifically responsible for the promotion of mortals. Zhang Yazi came to be regarded as the incarnation of the God of the Literati, and the Yazi Shrine in Zitong County was gradually elevated to become the Palace of the Literati God, and subse-

CHUNYANG HALL OF THE SOUTHERN SACRED MOUNTAIN.

quently the founding temple of hundreds of Literati God Temples across the country. In Daoist temples, the image of the God of the Literati is similar to that of emperors. In many stories and depictions, he rides a white donkey, and consorts with two boys, one of whom is a deaf person, called the Heavenly Deaf One; the other dumb, and called the Earthly Mute. The reason he is aided by the deaf and mute boys is that the affairs he is involved in are highly secret, and not allowed to be revealed. The one who can speak cannot hear, while the one who can hear cannot speak, so no one can ascertain the true nature of these secret affairs.

Five Element Emperors. These are five celestial gods representing the five directions: the Green Emperor in the east, the White Emperor in the west, the Red Emperor in the south, the Black Emperor in the north, and the Yellow Emperor in the center. They are a part of early religion and cosmological theory inherited by Daoism. According to Daoism, the Five Element Emperors were primordial, and when the universe split into heaven and earth, they transformed into five elements. They represent the five planets in the sky, guiding the celestial gods; the five sacred mountains on earth, ruling the earth gods; the five internal organs in human body, commanding the gods of the body. As mentioned earlier, they have their own images as well: the Green Dragon in the east, the White Tiger in the west, the Red Phoenix in the south, the Black Turtle-Snake in the north, and the Yellow Emperor in the center. The entire world consists of Five Elements, Five Directions, and Five Sacred Mountains. Therefore the Altar of Earth in Beijing, now located in Zhongshan Park, was composed of green, red, white, black, and yellow clay during the Qing Dynasty. It was the royal temple where sacrifices were offered to the Gods of the Earth, and its altar is symbolically the center of the entire country. Perhaps because the meanings of the Five Element Gods were too various to give each a definite name, there are four to seven titles for each god.

God of War. In Chinese his name is Xuanwu or Zhenwu, literally meaning Dark General or Perfect General, because he is the God of the Northern Lunar Mansions, the Black God of the North among the Five Element Gods. His status was not too important until the

A GOD OF WALLS AND MOATS.

14th or 15th century when the Black God of the North gradually grew prosperous, and was endowed with control over exorcisms, blessings, and protections. In 1403, Prince Zhudi of the Ming Dynasty raised a rebellion against his nephew, Emperor Jianwen, and usurped the throne. In order to justify his usurpation with what would appear as the will of higher powers, he had his subordinates fabricate a tale saying that the North God helped him defeat his nephew on the battlefield.

Soon after the coronation, he
launched large-scale constructions on Mount Wudang, resulting in many temples dedicated
to the God of War, whom he
ordered his people to worship.
Thus after this time the God of
War became a prominent Daoist
deity. Many scholars propose
that this trend was related to the
desire for protection stirred up
by repeated invasions from
northern nomads at that time.
In addition, some scholars
believe that China's highly
developed seafaring technology
during 15th century also

VILLAGE GODS.

enhanced the prosperity of the North God, because the north is the
direction that correlates with water in the five elements theory; the
God of the North is thus also the God of Water, therefore the god
of many people who depend upon the sea. In Foshan City,
Guangdong Province, there is still an early temple dedicated to the
God of the North that many overseas Chinese tourists visit to pray
for safe homeward journeys.

According to Daoist scriptures, the God of the North was originally a prince of the Pure Happy Kingdom, but he had no desire
to succeed to the throne. Instead he swore to kill all demons in the

GUANDI HALL OF THE GREAT PURITY PALACE. SHENYANG PROVINCE.

world, and went to Mount Taihe to cultivate Dao. After he had mastered Dao, he was sent by the Jade Emperor to guard the north. The Jade Emperor renamed Mount Taihe as Mount Wudang, whose name is interpreted to mean that "no one can hold this post except Zhenwu." He usually takes the image of a man wearing long flowing hair with black armor and clothing, stepping on a turtle-snake statue with bare feet.

Gods of the Five Sacred Mountains. These are gods that Daoism has taken over from early nature worship. According to ancient texts, the character for *yue* for peak (of a mountain), was originally the title for the officials in charge of mountains. Much later, the mountains took the name of their managers. Among numerous rituals related to mountain worship, only those for the Five Sacred Mountains were adapted to accord with the five elements theory. It was believed that because there are five planets in the sky, there are also five mountains corresponding to them. The descriptions of them as the immortal lands also shaped the concept of the Five Sacred Mountains.

Even before religious Daoism came into being, the First Emperor (Qinshi Huangdi) had already traveled to Mount Tai in 219 BCE to offer sacrifices to Heaven and Earth. Han Emperor Wu, escorted by a large band of followers, traveled first to Mount Song and Mount Hua, and later, in 110 BCE, to Mount Tai and Mount Heaven's Pillar for the same purpose. Han Emperor Wu had given an imperial edict to confirm Mount Tai as the Eastern Sacred Mountain, Mount Heaven's Pillar as the Southern Sacred Mountain (later replaced by Mount Heng in Hunan Province), Mount Hua as the Western Sacred Mountain, Mount Heng as the Northern Sacred Mountain and Mount Song as the Central Sacred Mountain; this edict also prescribed the sacrificial systems and liturgies for these mountains, which from that time on were granted superior status to all other mountains.

Having gradually matured from generation to generation, the sacrificial liturgies for the Five Sacred Mountains became imperial celebrations, and since ancient times, the Five Sacred Mountains have been considered Daoist paradises of retreat and cultivation.

The Gods of Sacred Mountains were in fact crowned as kings during the Tang Dynasty (618–907). According to *Compilation of Important Books in the Daoist Canon*, the God of the Eastern Sacred

A GOD OF WEALTH.

Mountain was honored as King of Heavenly Navel ("navel" here representing the center of heaven), the God of the Southern Sacred Mountain as King of Heavenly Management, the God of the Western Sacred Mountain as King of the Gold Heaven, the God of the Northern Sacred Mountain as King of Heavenly Safety, the God of the Central Sacred Mountain as King of Central Heaven. All of these deities commanded thousands of immortal officials and fairy maids, and watched over their various domains. They were further elevated to emperors during the Song Dynasty (960–1279). The Emperor of the Eastern Sacred Mountain is dressed in a plain green robe, rides a green dragon, commands 5900 subordinate deities, and determines human birth and death. All persons who have recently died must receive judgment by him, and he is the commander-in-chief of all ghosts. He has a daughter, named Princess Azure Clouds, who is benevolent and is the goddess one prays to when hoping for children.

The King of the Southern Sacred Mountain wears a plain red robe, rides a red dragon, and commands 7700 immortals. The King of the Western Sacred Mountain wears a plain white robe, rides a white dragon, and commands 4100 attendants and maids. The King of the Northern Sacred Mountain wears a plain black robe, rides a black dragon, and commands 7000 attendants and maids. The King of the Central Sacred Mountain wears a plain yellow robe, rides a yellow drag-on, and commands 30,000 attendants and maids.

WOODEN STATUE OF DIVINE GENERAL WANG.

Gods of Walls and Moats. These deities also come from ancient ritual practices inherited by Daoism. They are gods of towns and cities who have been ubiquitous in China since the 15th century; almost every town has a god of its own. They are all known historical figures, some meritorious officials or generals, some famous doctors or virtuous persons. Their role is to oversee and guard the lives of those in their realms and to report to the Heavenly Court on a regular basis in order to ensure that humans are doing their part to keep the balance of *yin* and *yang* in harmony.

Gods of Villages. In a manner similar to God of Walls and Moats, these deities have developed from rituals to worship the farmland around rural villages. Before Gods of Towns dominated in China, land worship had a hierarchy of deities conforming strictly to social structure, in which the emperor, kings, dukes, officials, and common people were allowed to worship only the land gods within their domains; the highest land deity was the Earthly Queen of the Four Imperial Ones. Ranked lower than Town Gods, the Gods of Villages have been very popular as grassroots deities since the 14th century, during the Ming dynasty. Some scholars speculate that this change came about as a result of an imperial edict, ostensibly because the first emperor of the Ming dynasty was born in a Village God shrine. The image of the Village God is that of a simply clothed, smiling, white-bearded man. His wife, the Grandma of the Village, looks like any old lady who might live next door.

God of the Kitchen. There are two points of view regarding the origin of this popular deity: one theory proposes that it derives from the ancient worship of fire, and that the God of Fire, Zhurong, and the discoverer of fire utilization, Emperor Yan (*yan* means hot) have been conflated to become a God of the Kitchen; the other theory holds that it developed from a sacrifice to memorialize old women, who since ancient times who have cooked food for people. Daoist tradition is apparently based on the latter explanation, since its God of the Kitchen is called the Old Lady of Kunlun or the Old Lady of Fire Seed. There are actually five Kitchen Gods, one for each of the five directions: the Eastern Green Kitchen God, the Southern Red Kitchen God, the Western White Kitchen God, the Northern Black Kitchen God and the Yellow Central Kitchen God. In later times, the duties of the Kitchen God have been extended to becoming the protector of the whole family in which she resides, and also being the messenger sent by the Jade Emperor to every family who reports the good and evil deeds of family members. The dates of making this report vary from place to place, as do the customs associated with it. Rituals for Reporting Day include burning the statue of the Kitchen God on the 23rd day of the 12th month, symbolizing sending the Kitchen God to Heaven, then inaugurating a new figure to welcome her back on the 30th day of the same month. Many people also fill the statue's mouth with sweet glutinous rice, bribing her to report more praises than rebukes; other families eat candy to express the same meaning.

Gods of Wealth. These are also household deities who control fortune and success. There are Military Wealth Gods, such as Zhao Xuantan and Guandi, and Civilian Wealth Gods, such as Bigan and Fanli. "Civilian" or "military" here designates the secular professions these historical figures used to perform, but has nothing to do with their divine functions.

The most popular Wealth God is Zhao Xuantan, also known as Zhao Gongming, or Marshal Zhaogong. It is reported that he was formerly a superintendent-general of ghosts in the service of the Jade Emperor, and also a god of the plague; afterwards he was subdued by Celestial Master Zhang and was installed as Zhengyi Esoteric Altar Marshal because of his effective help in guarding Zhang's elixir stove. It is reported that he is dressed in a black robe with black armor, rides a fierce black tiger, holds a steel whip, as well as balls that can pacify the sea or be used as weapons. Zhao

Xuantan also carries a dragon-binding cable. What is especially important is that he commands four aides who help people with business endeavors.

Guandi, or Emperor Guan, originally named Guanyu, was a general in the Shu State during the Three Kingdoms Period (220–265). He is worshiped as the God of Military Wealth because when he whenever he mounted or dismounted his horse in the camp of Caocao, the latter would make offerings of gold to him to engage his services. However, loyal to another leader, Guandi did not accept the gold; his loyalty serves as a model of "attracting money by following the principles of Dao." Today the figure of Guandi is still seen everywhere, from businesses to household shrines.

Bigan was the righteous and upright uncle of King Zhou of Shang, the despotic last emperor of the Shang Dynasty (ca. 1600–ca. 1100 BCE). Displeased by his nephew's atrocities, he spoke out against him; his nephew retaliated by cutting out his heart. A later version of the tale held that Bigan cut out his own heart, and placed it in front of the King in order to shame him. Whichever story, Bigan did not die, but instead walked proudly out of the court to hand out money to the people. He became a popular God of Wealth among the masses because he truly had no heart of his own; he was indeed selfless and impartial. It was believed that if a businessman fixed his scales to cheat customers, Bigan would rebalance the scale to protect them; he is thus also the symbol of honest business practices.

Fanli was a minister of the Yue State during the Spring and Autumn and Warring States periods. However, he chose to abdicate his position, conceal his true identity, and retreat to the state of Qi (now Shandong) to practice business. He was very capable in financial matters, having made a fortune three times, each time distributing the money to the poor. He was called Old Man of Porcelain and Pearl, perhaps he participated in these two businesses. He is a model businessman and also revered as God of Wealth.

Divine General Wang. Wangshan, the Guardian God of Daoism, was a historical figure during the reign of Emperor Huizong of the Song dynasty. He was originally a member of the bodyguard of the Jade Emperor's Sacred Heaven Palace, and was later appointed by the Jade Emperor to be the Town God of Huaiyin Prefecture in Jiangsu Province. One day, when Perfected Man Sa passed by the temple of Wang, the local governor drove him away at the request of Wang. Mortified and furious, Sa used his magic to burn down Wang's temple, rendering Wang homeless. Wang had no choice but to follow Sa for more than ten years as a subordinate. During the Yongle era (1403–1425) of the Ming Dynasty, a Daoist from Hangzhou claimed to have acquired Wang's mystic techniques of divination. He was so well known that everyone in Beijing had heard of him, and Emperor Yongle summoned him for consultation time and time again. The emperor ordered one temple each be built for Sa and Wang to the west of the Forbidden City. Whenever he went out for a battle, the emperor would take a cane statue of Wang with him. In the Xuande era (1426–1436) of the Ming, Wang was royally installed as the Perfect Master of Great Favor, and his shrine was enlarged and renamed the Great Favor Hall. In the Chenghua era (1464–1488) of the Ming, the Fire Virtue Temple, home to Wang's hall, was called Sacred Attestation Palace. There were annual celebrations on the emperor's birthday, lunar New Year, the winter solstice; on those days and others memorializing his famous predictions, ministers were sent to offer sacrifices. Since then, Wangshan has become the guardian god in the first hall of Daoist temples, and is honored as Divine General Wang.

Divine General Wang has a red face with a long beard and three eyes; he wears a red robe with gold armor, and stands on the wheel of wind and fire, with finger charms in his left hand and a steel whip in his right. He is upright, never falls for flatterers, hates evil like an enemy, and supervises all good and evil deeds on both heaven and earth. So there is a saying: "Three eyes penetrate all things under heaven, one whip arouses every person in the world."

This chapter has presented a brief summary of the many characters making up the colorful Daoist pantheon of deities. Readers should not be overly concerned about keeping track of their various origins, groupings, rankings, and responsibilities. A thorough understanding of these seemingly countless deities is not necessary to a general comprehension of the Daoist religion.

CHAPTER 5

Daoist Temples and Sacred Places

The Development of Daoist Temples and their Organizational Systems

Daoist temples are where Daoists consecrate and celebrate their deities, conduct rituals and ceremonies, and dwell. The earliest Daoist groups did not have temples. For quite a long time after Zhang Daoling founded his sect, the places of Daoist activity were political centers, meditation rooms, and communal hostels. Political centers contained the offices of Daoist officials and their meeting rooms for what were, at the time, small, localized theocracies. Meditation rooms were places where followers came to be cured, meditate, and commune with deities, while communal hostels were where local communities accommodated visiting followers and descended deities.

Nowadays Daoist temples are variously called *guan* (originally meaning a watchtower on either side of a gate) or *gong* (originally a palace), *tai* (terrace), *dong* (cave, but also meaning "insight"), *tang* (hall), *yuan* (courtyard), and *miao* (temple). It is said that immortals dwell on *tai* or in *guan,* which were originally made of gold and white jade. What is considered to be the earliest Daoist temple, Louguantai, in Zhouzhi County, Shaanxi Province, was originally the astronomical observatory of Yinxi, one of Laozi's disciples and a local governor of the Zhou dynasty; its name therefore contains

A HALL FOR GUEST AT THE CELESTIAL MASTERS MANSION. JIANGXI PROVINCE.

lou (storied building), *guan* and *tai*. This was where Laozi reportedly wrote and first taught the *Daode Jing*. Emperor Wu of the Han dynasty, who ruled in the last half of the 2nd century BCE, believed in immortal doctrines. When he learned that immortals liked to reside in high buildings, he ordered the construction of the Feilian Guan in the capital of Changan (now Xi'an), and the Yanshou Guan in the suburbs, for their amusement. From these precedents *guan* came to be used in the names of Daoist temples; centuries later, Emperor Wu of the Northern Zhou dynasty (561–582) ordered all Daoist temples to incorporate *guan* in their names. During the Tang dynasty, the imperial family, surnamed Li, claimed Laozi as their ancestor. After that all temples in honor of

THE YONGLE GONG (ETERNAL HAPPINESS PALACE). RUICHENG COUNTY, SHANXI PROVINCE.

Laozi were renamed as palaces. In later centuries, as more and more immortals were praised and conceived of as emperors, more and more temples came to be called palaces, and *gongguan* has become the general name for Daoist temples.

The architectural styles of Daoist temples has varied over the centuries, depending up their locales and the deities associated with them, until the 13th century, when the overall layout of all Daoist temples became more uniform. Most medium to large temples today typically consist of a gate, bell tower, drum tower, Divine General Wang Hall, Central Hall, Jade Emperor Hall, Three Pure Ones Hall, and sect founder hall. Many temples also have preserved relics of historical figures.

All temples established a central administrative system: every temple had a well-trained and highly revered abbot, in turn aided by a dean to oversee all administration. Daoist officials were divided into the following categories: liaison officials, hall managers, preachers, treasurers, cooks, warehouse managers, disciplinary officials, and dormitory managers. Some large temples had several assistants for each section. There were strict rules and practices for each official position, and any violation was punished.

Since the establishment of the People's Republic of China in 1949, temples have done away with feudal management systems, and assumed democratic management. Temples are administrated by a Democratic Management Committee whose members are chosen through regular elections. Committee members, through group discussion, decide all important affairs. Some temples have also set up modern institutions such as receptionist offices, administrative offices, and security offices, although the basic temple functions have not changed. Though Zhengyi Dao masters have families and homes, they usually live very close to their temples, where nearly all religious activity takes place. They are part of the temple's democratic administration and obey its principles.

THE SACRED PLACES OF DAOISM

There are more than 4500 Daoist temples in mainland China. Most of them are not only the places of daily religious activity, but also important cultural sites and tourist attractions. Among them the most important ones are the following:

The Five Sacred Mountains of Daoism. Mount Tai is the Eastern Sacred Mountain and the paramount of the five sacred mountain. It is located among the counties of Tai'an, Licheng, and Changqing in Shandong Province. The altitude of the highest peak is 1545 meters. The worship of Mount Tai supposedly originated during the 20th century BCE, during the Xia dynasty. Emperors of all past dynasties went there to offer sacrifices. The Temple of Mount Tai, located at the foot of the mountain, is the central temple for the

MORNING MIST AT AZURE CLOUD TEMPLE, MOUNT TAI. SHANDONG PROVINCE.

God of the East. The whole compound occupies 98,000 square meters. The central hall is 22.3 meters high, 48.7 meters long, and 19.8 meters wide, and is covered with yellow-glazed tiles, giving it the flavor of a palace. There is a large-scale fresco on its inner walls, 3.3 meters high and 63 meters long, depicting the scene of an inspection tour of the Eastern God escorted by more than six hundred people. It is reported to be a work of the 12th century, with great artistic and cultural value.

Azure Cloud Temple, located on top of Mount Tai, enshrines the princess of the Eastern God in a building dating back to the Song Dynasty. The ridge of the roof, like the beak of some great bird, as well as the eave bells of the central hall are made of bronze, while the tiles on the halls of the wings are made of iron. There are two bronze steles fashioned in the 15th century in the courtyard. Other Daoist buildings are Queen Mother Hall, Mother of the Big Dipper Hall, Ascending Hall, and Jade Emperor Hall.

The Southern Sacred Mountain. This is Mount Heng, located in Hengshan County, Hunan Province, with a total of 72 peaks, of which the highest is

THE EASTERN COURTYARD OF JADE SPRING MONASTERY, MOUNT HUA. SHAANXI PROVINCE.

MOUNT HUA, THE WESTERN SACRED MOUNTAIN, SHAANXI PROVINCE.

Zhurong Peak (1290 meters). Heng Shan is famous for its beautiful natural scenery, and is recognized as the most gorgeous sacred mountain in China. It has been a Daoist sacred mountain since ancient times, when it is said that Laozi visited it, bestowed the better part of *Daode Jing* onto King Zhurong, and taught him how to rule under the guidance of Dao. The Queen Mother also came here to teach Madam Wei how to practice cultivating herself in the Jin Dynasty. It is recorded that 109 famous Daoists have practiced cultivation at Mount Heng since the Han dynasty, among whom nine succeeded in achieving Dao. King Zhurong himself is also the God of the Southern Sacred Mountain. The Temple of the Southern God is at the foot of Mount Heng, construction of which began in the Tang dynasty; it has undergone countless repairs and enlargements over succeeding dynasties. The present building was renovated in 1882, during the Qing dynasty. The whole compound occupies 98,500 square meters; the central building is 22 meters high, containing 72 pillars symbolizing the 72 peaks of Mount Heng. The outer buildings include the Sleeping Palace, the Royal Study, and the Winding Dragon Pavilion. In 1997, the Daoist Association of the Southern Sacred Mountain reconstructed the Chunyang Hall, Benevolent Longevity Hall, Master Lao Hall, the Jade Emperor Hall and the Medicine King Hall, adding 7900 square meters to this compound, making it a magnificent site displaying ancient architectural styles.

Other Daoist buildings on the Southern Sacred Mountain are Xuandu (Immortal's Capital) Temple on the middle of the mountainside, Founder Master's Temple at Heaven's Southern Gate, and

Yellow Court Temple at the foot of Sages Meeting Peak. Most of these buildings were destroyed by long wars before 1949 and during the Cultural Revolution (1966–1976). They were rebuilt and even enlarged during the 1980s under the efforts of the local Daoist association. The Yellow Court Temple is said to be the last cultivation place of Madam Wei, in front of which there is a giant rock, said to be her spot of ascension.

The Western Sacred Mountain. This honor belongs to Mount Hua in the south of Huayin County. In Chinese *hua* means flower, or splendor. It is named Flower Mountain because the five peaks together make it look like a lotus. The altitude of the highest peaks is around 2200 meters. It has always been famous for its rugged slopes, and is recognized as the most dangerous sacred mountain in China. Many famous Daoists have meditated and practiced cultivation on this mountain, leaving numerous sites associated with their presence, such as Xiyuan (Western Element) Cave, Huashan Cave, Lotus Cave, Jade Emperor's Cave, Supreme Cave, Congratulating Longevity Cave, Greeting Sunrise Cave, and Xiyi's Cave. The

MOUNT HENG, THE SOUTHERN SACRED MOUNTAIN. HUNAN PROVINCE.

Temple of the Western God is at the eastern end of the town at the mountain foot. Its building was initiated during the reign of Emperor Wu of the Han dynasty (140–89 BCE), reconstructed in 576 of the Northern Zhou dynasty, in 836 during the Tang dynasty, and again in 961 during the Northern Song dynasty. The existing buildings are the results of recent reconstruction in the Ming and Qing dynasties. The grand central hall was a palace that would accommodate visiting emperors. The steles in the courtyard, valuable cultural relics, are the actual records of this temple's history.

The Jade Spring Monastery is at the mouth of the northern valley. It is recorded that Chentuan, a famous Daoist monk of the Song dynasty, practiced cultivation there. After his ascension, his

MOUNT HENG, THE NORTHERN SACRED MOUNTAIN. SHANXI PROVINCE.

disciples built Xiyi Shrine as the memorial (Xiyi is the honorific of Chentuan, and means "diffuse and remote"). After several expansions during the Qing dynasty, it was renamed Jade Spring Monastery. In the 1980s, the Daoist Association of Mount Hua added the newly built cloister and rock garden to the delicate ancient compound. This temple compound has been arranged in three sections. The middle section highlights Xiyi Shrine; the eastern line contains Huatuo's Tomb (Huatuo was a famous doctor of the Three Kingdoms period), cloister, and the Twelve Caves; the western line contains the stone boat and Xiyi's Cave. The eastern yard is only passage to the mountain. It used to be a private school during the Ming dynasty before Daoists transformed it into a place for religious practice in 1714, during the Qing dynasty; therefore the place is quite small. The major hall consists of only three rooms, within which the Black Lady of the Empyrean is enshrined.

The Mountain Guard's Palace, also called the Upper Palace, is located in the valley among Jade Maiden Peak, Lotus Peak, and Goose Perching Peak. Enshrined here is the God of the West. There is a well in the yard, which is believed to lead to the Jade Spring Monastery.

Emerald Cloud Palace is on the top of Lotus Peak. It is the temple of the Third Holy Mother and her son, Chenxiang. There is a giant rock beside the temple, with a crevice in it, which looks as if it had been cut apart by a huge axe. It is associated with a legend about Chenxiang saving his mother. According to the story, the goddess in the temple was a heavenly fairy maiden, but she could not bear her loneliness. So she descended to the mundane world, married without permission, and gave birth to Chenxiang. Her second eldest brother, who was a general of Jade Emperor, was sent down to capture her and placed the giant rock upon her, trapping her. Having grown into a strong man, Chenxiang split the giant rock and freed his mother.

The Northern Sacred Mountain. Mount Heng is in Hunyuan County, Shanxi Province; the altitude of the highest peak is 2017 meters. The Northern Sacred Mountain was originally Mount Damao in Quyang County, Hebei Province; however, in 1403, when Ming Emperor Chengzhu moved the capital from Nanjing to Beijing, he thought it unreasonable to worship Mount Damao as the Northern Sacred Mountain, because it is actually south of Beijing. He ordered the title of Northern Sacred Mountain transferred from Mount Damao to Mount Heng. However, it was not convenient to offer sacrifices to Mount Heng because the transportation to Hunyuan was difficult and marauding northern tribes often roamed the area; thus rituals were still held at Mount Damao, offering sacrifices indirectly to Mount Heng. It was not possible for memorial sacrifices to be held in Hunyuan until Emperor Shunzhi's reign during the Qing dynasty.

Today the large central hall of the original Northern God Temple built during Yuan dynasty remains intact. It is the largest building in China existing from the Yuan dynasty, containing huge frescos on the four walls that are Yuan works in the manner of the great Tang painter Wu Daozi. It was during the Zhou dynasty that the mountain worship activities first took place here and there were already a good number of practitioners of self-cultivation

YAOCAN PAVILION AND THE MIDDLE HEAVENLY TOWER OF SONG SHAN, THE CENTRAL SACRED
MOUNTAIN. HENAN PROVINCE.

dwelling on the mountain during the Han dynasty. In the 7th century, during the Tang dynasty, Daoism on Mount Heng was quite popular and prosperous. However, most of the extant Daoist buildings were constructed during the Ming dynasty.

God Heng Hall, also called Primordial Spirit Palace, is the temple of the Northern God, as well as his four ministers and four marshals. It was constructed in 1501 during the Ming dynasty. Other attached buildings include a temple library and a bell and drum tower. There are also more than ten steles in the yard, among them an iron stele erected in 1324 during the Yuan dynasty.

Northwest of God Heng Hall is Gathering Immortals Hall, in which the Three Constellation Gods of Happiness, Success, and Longevity and other immortals from various celestial ministries are enshrined. To the east of God Heng Hall is Jade Emperor Pavilion and Royal Stele Pavilion. Sleeping Palace was initiated on the Supreme Peace Terrace during the reign of the Great Wu Emperor of the Northern Wei dynasty (424–452), which used to be the central hall of the Northern God Temple. The extant building was constructed during the Ming dynasty, and is dedicated to the Northern God and his queen.

The Central Sacred Mountain. Mount Song is in Dengfeng County, Henan Province; the altitude of the highest peak is 1440 meters. It has been the object of mountain worship since ancient times. It is reported that in 110 BCE when Emperor Wu of the Han dynasty visited the mountain, he heard the forest winds and thought they sounded like throngs hailing "Long live the Emperor!" He was so delighted that he issued bans on cutting trees and grass, ordained it as a sacred mountain, and renamed it Long

ENTRY GATE OF WHITE CLOUD TEMPLE, BEIJING.

Life Mountain. Upon the summit of the mountain he built a Long Life Pavilion, and at its base, a Long Life Watchtower. Based on this story, laudatory shouting of such good wishes for the emperor came to be called *shanhu* (literally, "mountain shouting"). Empress Wu Zetian of the Tang dynasty ascended and consecrated this sacred mountain on two occasions, in 688 and in 696. It was she who renamed the county Dengfeng, which means "to climb" (*deng*) and "to consecrate" (*feng*).

Today most of the mountain temples have been converted to Buddhist places of worship, but the Central God Temple at the mountain's eastern foot remains and is the major Daoist temple in the area. It has been built, repaired, rebuilt, and expanded throughout many dynasties; it was renovated nine times during the Qing dynasty alone. The present monastic compound spreads more than 110,000 square meters, embracing more than 300 halls and pavilions, as well as a library and a dormitory. As the central building, Junji (Extremely Craggy) Hall was rebuilt in 1653 of Qing dynasty, was partially destroyed by Japanese air raids, and restored after 1949. The inner statue of the Central God is 5 meters high. In the yard there are more than 330 ancient cypress trees from the Han, Tang, and Song Dynasties, and more than ten ancient steles. Especially rare and valuable Daoist relics are the four "iron titans" standing in front of the Chongsheng gate.

The Three Founder Temples of the Quanzhen Sect. These are: White Cloud Temple in Beijing, Eternal Happiness Palace, and Double Yang Palace, the latter both in Shaanxi.

White Cloud Temple lies
outside of Xibianmen in
Beijing. It was initiated as
Tianchang Temple for Laozi in
739, during the Tang dynasty,
and rebuilt as Taiji Palace in
1203, during the Jin dynasty. In
1224, when the founder of
Dragon Gate Sect, a sub-sect of
Quanzhen, came back to
Beijing from the long journey to
meet with Genghis Khan, he
resided at Taiji Palace. Since he
had been honored as an
Everlasting-Spring Perfect Man

MING DYNASTY WOODEN STATUE OF LU
DONGBIN, FOUNDER OF THE YONGLE GONG.

by the Khan, his temple was renamed as Everlasting-Spring Palace.
He stayed in the temple for three years engaged in missionary work
before he passed away and was buried under the Pliable Residence
Hall of the temple.

Everlasting-Spring Palace thus became one of the founder tem-
ples of the Perfect Realization Denomination. It was destroyed by
flames of war at the end of the Yuan dynasty and rebuilt during the
Ming dynasty. In 1443, during the Ming dynasty, Emperor Yingzong
bestowed on the temple a tablet inscribed on with a new name,
White Cloud Temple, the name still used today. White Cloud
Temple was very prosperous during the Qing dynasty. The famous
Abbot Wang Changyue held ordination assemblies there three

times, in which he converted and ordained more than a thousand Daoist monks. When Emperor Kangxi was a prince he visited White Cloud Temple to receive its Daoist teachings; subsequently its landholdings increased greatly. Today the complex occupies more than 60,000 square meters, and contains more than 10,000 square meters of buildings, including the halls of the Divine General, Mother of the Big Dipper, Three Elements Gods, Wealth Gods, Jade Emperor, Three Pure Ones, Four Imperial Ones, and numerous ancillary buildings and structures, such Blocking Wind Bridge, a Bell and Drum Tower, the Commandment-Receiving

DETAIL OF A FRESCO AT THE ETERNAL HAPPINESS PALACE (YONGLE GONG). SHANXI PROVINCE.

Platform, and numerous gardens. At present it is the headquarters of the Chinese Taoist Association (CTA) and the Chinese Daoist College, founded in 1957 and 1991, respectively.

Eternal Happiness Palace, formally called the Chunyang Palace of Longevity, lies in Ruicheng County, Shaanxi Province, the birthplace of Lu Dongbin. Chunyang, meaning "pure *yang*," is Lu Dongbin's Daoist name. After Lu passed away, the natives of his hometown rebuilt his family house and made it a shrine to Lu. Having been expanded as a Daoist monastery under the order of the Yuan emperor, it was named Eternal Happiness, or Yongle, after the name of the town, and is one of the founder temples of the Quanzhen Sect. In 1959, while the Sanmen Gorge Dam was being constructed, this temple was moved to present day Longquan Village. The major buildings include Dragon Tiger Hall, Three Pure Ones Hall, Chunyang Hall, and Chongyang Hall, all of which are Yuan dynasty constructions. The most famous relics are the frescos on the walls, which are masterpieces of Chinese art. Taking 120 years to complete, they cover 960 square meters. The Pilgrimage to the Origin fresco of Three Pure Ones Hall is 94.68 meters long and 4.26 meters high, and in its 286 figures of various kinds, one can see the vivid depiction of the pilgrimage of numerous immortals to the Heavenly Sage of the Preexistence. The work has been praised as "the crowning achievement of Eastern art" and is on the list of National Cultural Relic Sites.

Chongyang Palace, formally called Chongyang Palace of Longevity (often abbreviated as Founder's Temple), is at Liu Jiang Village, Hu County, Shaanxi Province. It was the birthplace of Wang

LAOZI HALL AT THE LOUGUANTAI, WHICH FEATURES A STELE OF THE *DAODE JING* IN THE COURTYARD.
SHAANXI PROVINCE.

Chongyang. After Wang Chongyang passed away in 1170, his disciple Wang Chuyi took the corpse back to Hu County, and established a shrine at the site where Wang first practiced his faith. Afterwards, his disciples begged for donations to expand the temple, which is recognized a founder temple of the Quanzhen sect. At the zenith of its expansion during the Yuan dynasty it contained 5000 rooms. Today, the compound has shrunk to less than 8,000 square meters. Although most of the buildings, such as the Master Lao Hall and Founder Hall, were rebuilt during the Ming and Qing dynasties, there are still more than thirty steles dating back to the Yuan dynasty, inscribed in both Chinese and Mongolian, precious relics of Daoist history.

The Earliest Daoist Temple.
Louguantai rests is at the foot of
Mount Zhongnan in Zhouzhi
County, Shaanxi Province. It is
said that it was established in
the 10th century BCE during
the Zhou dynasty. It was then
the astrological observatory of
Yinxi, a local Zhou official, and
was called Caoloutai, meaning
Thatched Pavilion Terrace.
When Yinxi observed that there
were purple clouds coming
from the east, he was sure that a
great sage was about to appear.
He therefore abandoned his
official position and went to

THREE HEAVEN GATE ON MOUNT MAO. JIANGSU
PROVINCE.

wait at Hangu Pass. Soon afterward Laozi arrived, riding a black
ox. Laozi was invited into the thatched tower, and instructed Yinxi
in the contents of the *Daode Jing* and other skills. Thereafter
Louguantai was also called Sermon Terrace. The First Emperor of
Qin was entranced with theories of immortality as well as with
Laozi, and had a temple built to the south of the tower, called Pure
Temple. Emperor Wu of the Han added a temple to the north side
of the tower, called Expecting Immortal Palace. In the Tang and
Song dynasties, emperors who fervently believed in Daoism con-
tributed to the expansion of Louguantai into a huge monastery,

considered at the time one of the finest Daoist centers in China. Famous Daoist masters flocked there, among them the greatly revered master of the Quanzhen sect, Lu Dongbin, who practiced cultivation and achieved Dao there.

Tang emperors, who regarded themselves as the descendants of Laozi, appointed Louguantai as the Ancestor Sage Palace, the temple of their royal and sagely ancestor. They even assigned lands to the temple as they would to royal relatives. These events are recorded on the remnant stele inscribed by Ou Yangxiu, a great scholar of Tang. Another extant stele tells the story of the close relationship between the Tang court and Louguantai: One night in 741, Emperor Xuanzong dreamed of Laozi. Thereupon a jade statue was excavated from the spot on the southeastern hill indicated

A TEMPLE ON MOUNT MAO, JIANGSU PROVINCE.

by the dream. Meeting God Temple was thereupon ordered by the emperor to be built on the hill, which was renamed Sacred Presence Hill.

An emperor of the Song dynasty renamed the temple Heaven-Abiding, Empire-Reviving Temple, and lauded Laozi as Supreme Emperor of the Primordial Chaos. There are two steles from the Song dynasty by the famous calligrapher, Mifei, and the great scholar, Su Dongpo. However Louguantai has been destroyed and rebuilt repeatedly since the Yuan dynasty. Important extant buildings are Laozi Temple, Divine General Hall, Mother of the Big Dipper Hall, the Library, Sermon Terrace, and the tomb of Laozi.

JIANFU TEMPLE OF MOUNT QINGCHENG. SICHUAN PROVINCE.

Birthplace of the Supreme Pure Sect. Mount Mao lies across the four counties of Jurong, Jintan, Lishui, and Liyang. It is recorded that three brothers, named Maoying, Maogu, and Maozhong, came to this mountain, originally Mount Juqu, to practice cultivation techniques in 82 BCE, during the reign of Emperor Zhao of the Han

ETERNAL DAO TEMPLE (CELESTIAL MASTER'S CAVE) AT MOUNT QINGCHENG. SICHUAN PROVINCE.

dynasty. The brothers became known for their skills in curing people with herbal remedies. After the three brothers attained Dao, the mountain was renamed Mount Mao in their honor, and the three highest peaks designated Mount Mao One, Mount Mao Two, and Mount Mao Three. Since then Mount Mao has always been one of the great retreats of Daoists, many of whose fame spread wide. During the Jin dynasty, the great Daoist Gehong practiced cultivation techniques there and composed his great work *Baopuzi*; in 364, Xumi, Xusun (the son of Xumi), and Yangxi founded the Shangqing Sect, whose major god is the Heavenly Sage of the Pre-existence; in 488, a famous Daoist theorist, Tao Hongjin, wrote his *Instruction of Truth* and *Catalogue of the Daoist Pantheon* there.

MOUNT WUDANG, GREAT HARMONY MOUNTAIN. HUBEI PROVINCE.

Many buildings have been constructed in this complex since the Tang dynasty, making Mount Mao one of the three great centers of Zhengyi Daoism. Daoists on Mount Mao have received countless favor from past emperors. For example, all forests and lands that used to be public were designated as the territory of the temple. After the 16th century, Quanzhen Daoists began to establish temples on the mountain as well, making it a sacred mountain shared by two Daoist denominations. In the 1930s, when the Japanese invaded eastern China, Mount Mao became a base of the Chinese Communist New Fourth Army. Daoists on the mountain actively supported the resistance, and some of them even joined the Communist Army. The Daoists on Mount Mao have made great contributions whilst suffering great losses. All temples on the mountain were burned by Japanese invaders and many Daoists were brutally slaughtered. In 1949, Daoists from all temples on the mountain organized an administrative group and began to rebuild temples. In 1963, the construction of Roof Palace along with its statues was completed on the highest peaks, and a consecration ceremony was held that year.

Daoist activities were forced to cease during the Cultural Revolution, and it was not until the 1980s when Daoist organizations were re-established and some important Daoist buildings and relics were rebuilt with government aid. Roof Palace, formally named The Highest Sky Complete Happiness Palace, was constantly restored from 1982 to 1998. Its major buildings include Divine General Hall, the Library, Great Original Jewel Hall, Holy Parents Hall, Three Heaven Gate, and Ascendance Terrace. Great Original

GREAT HARMONY PALACE, MOUNT WUDANG. HUBEI PROVINCE.

Jewel Hall is the central hall, within which are enshrined the Perfect Masters, along with the Three Maos, with carved stone busts of 45 deities and the memorial tablets of past famous Daoists who practiced cultivation techniques on Mount Mao. Holy Parents Hall was dedicated to the parents of the Three Maos. It is said Gehong used the ancient well in the yard to mix elixirs.

Original Tally Palace, constructed as a temple in the 8th century, is said to be the cultivation place of Tao Hongjin. Emperor Huizong of the Song dynasty renamed it Elemental Tally Palace, and granted it a jade seal; it was therefore also called Seal Palace. Most of the extant buildings were rebuilt in 1988, including Observatory Gate, Divine General Palace, Stele

Pavilion, Longevity Terrace, and Great Origin Jewel Palace. Observatory Gate used to be the astrological working place of Daoists. It is a stone building, 21.8 meter wide and 7.5 meter high, with three gates that were restored in 1987. Longevity Terrace used to be called the "Holy Terrace," as there specially designed liturgies were regularly held to seek the blessings of emperors and empresses during the Song and Yuan dynasties. The three-tiered blue-stone terrace was restored in 1992, and a stone boat was installed at the center of the top level. In the 1990s, the Daoist Association of Mount Mao constructed a 33-meter statue of Laozi on the adjacent slope, which has become a well-known symbol of Mount Mao.

Heavenly Origin Temple is said to be the elixir-making place of occult master Li Mingzhen of the Qin dynasty. In the 11th century (during the Yuan dynasty) it was expanded into a Quanzhen monastery. In 1993, it was renovated as the Perfect Realization Nunnery with several halls, in which the important relics are the Elixir Well of the Perfected Man Li Mingzhen, and the Tomb of Kang Youwei's Mother. (Kong Youwei is a famous modern Chinese politician and scholar.)

The Birthplace of Religious Daoism. At the eastern end of the Qionglai mountain range, Mount Qingcheng, literally Mount Green City, is in the southwest of Dujiang Weir City, Sichuan Province. With heavy forests and thirty-six peaks, it is recognized as the most serene sacred mountain in China. It used to be named Ghost City Mountain because local residents believed that ghosts lived there; however it was named Du Mountain during the Qin and Han dynasty. In 221 BCE, when the Qin Emperor united China, he ordered the offering of royal sacrifices to the 18 sacred mountains, among which he listed Du Mountain. As Governor of Shu Prefecture (under the Qin dynasty), Libin and his son initiated and presided over the construction of the world-famous irrigation works called Dujiang Weir, in the late Warring States period. Because Mount Qingcheng is the center of the area where Zhang Daoling founded his Daoist sect, early Daoist rituals was greatly influenced by customs of local minority tribes. Being the cradle of religious Daoism, all past generations of Celestial Masters and numerous other Daoists made pilgrimages to Mount Qingcheng.

The important extant structures include the Celestial Master Cave, Founder Master Hall, Supreme Pure Palace, Constructing Happiness Palace, Round Bright Palace, and Pure Jade Palace. Celestial Master's Cave, also known as the Eternal Dao Temple, is located on the 1,000 meter sloped terrace between White Cloud Brook and Crabapple Brook. It is a compound of 7200 square meters with halls of the Three Pure Ones, the Yellow Emperor, and the Three August Ones. There is actually a cave inside the Celestial Master Hall, hence the temple's name. It is a cave in which Zhang Daoling lived, within which an enshrined stone statue of Zhang Daoling remains from the Sui dynasty. It is a place all past Celestial Masters were required to visit. Founder Master Hall was dedicated to the famous priest Du Guangting of the Tang dynasty, who studied and wrote here, as well as Zhang Sanfeng of the Ming dynasty, a legendary master of Daoist cultivation and martial arts.

The famous general Feng Yuxiang lived in this hall during World War II, and left a stele in memory of the victory.

Shangqing Palace lies to the south of the terrace, construction of which was initiated during the Jin dynasty; it was rebuilt most recently in 1869. A temple stele is inscribed with the calligraphy of the former leader of the Nationalist Party, Jiang Jieshi (Chiang Kaishek). There are halls of the Three Pure Ones, the Jade Emperor, Confucius and Guandi, and the Eastern God. The Yin-Yang Wells in the yard are twin wells, one of which is square, shallow, and turbid, while the other is round, deep and clear. Numerous paintings and calligraphic works by the famous 20th-century artist Zhang Daqian (Chang Dai-ch'ien) are preserved here. The Master Lao Pavilion on the highest peak is a recent construction, with excellent views of the mountain scenery all around.

The Central Sacred Site for Emperor Zhenwu. Mount Wudang, also known as Mount Great Harmony, lies in Jun County, Hubei Province. With 72 peaks, 24 ravines, 11 caves, 9 springs, 9 wells and a 1612-meter crowning peak, the mountain's mystical beauty has long inspired myth and legend. Long before religious Daoism was founded, Mount Wudang had always been populated with occult masters, and after religious Daoism was developed, the site remained popular in the imagination of Daoists. It is from this mountain that Yinxi, Lu Dongbin, Sun Simiao, Chentuan, and Zhang Sanfeng poured fresh streams into the spiritual waters of Daoist history. It is said that Emperor Zhenwu practiced Daoist cultivation on the mountain for 42 years and then became immortal.

Since the 11th century legends about him have spread throughout the country, making Mount Wudang the central site of the God of the North, variously called the God of Water, Emperor Zhenwu, or the God of War. However this deity's functions were not confined to the aforementioned. He is also God of Fertility, God of Fortune, and even more important, is another embodiment of *taiji* (the Great Ultimate), directly related to Dao, and is therefore especially revered by alchemists.

Daoists on Mount Wudang have fused Confucianism and Buddhism with Daoism, upholding and promoting the Confucian virtues of loyalty and filial piety, and also practicing martial arts as part of cultivating good health. The fame of its Daoist inner martial arts is on par with that of Shaolin Temple's Buddhist outer martial arts. Daoist inner martial arts, such as *taiji quan* (shadow boxing), *bagua quan* (eight-trigram boxing) and Wudang sword fighting, put into practice Daoist theories of "overcoming the hard with the soft" and "controlling the moving with the still." They advocate the principles of "taking defense as purpose, attacking only when threatened, and relying completely on inner energy."

First constructed in the 7th century during the Tang dynasty, Daoist buildings on Mount Wudang have been destroyed and repaired repeatedly. In 1412, Emperor Zhudi of the Ming dynasty hosted the largest scale construction on Mount Wudang in order to repay the favor that the God of the North had conferred upon him. It took eight years to complete the 8 palaces, 2 temples, 36 shrines, and 72 caves. Since then it has been the center of worship of

Emperor Zhenwu. These buildings have been badly damaged by wars and disturbances over the past century, especially during the 1920s. In March of 1931, troops of the Red Army under Marshal Helong quartered at Mount Wudang, and received aid from local Daoists; after the Red Army departed they were suppressed cruelly by the Nationalist Party, and many Daoist leaders were killed.

The extant Daoist temples include Great Harmony Palace, Purple Sky Palace, Gold Roof Palace, Recover the Perfect Temple, and South Cliff Palace. Purple Sky Palace at the foot of Unfolded Flag Peak, which was initiated in 1413, is the largest temple on the mountain and the offices of the Mount Wudang Daoist Association. The buildings of the temple are aligned in three rows of which the eastern row constitutes the East Palace, the western row the West Palace and the middle row the halls of Dragon-Tiger, Ten-Directions, Purple Sky, and Parents. Dragon-Tiger Hall enshrines the Dragon and Tiger Protector, while Ten-Direction Hall enshrines the Divine General, along with a 9 meter high, 90-ton stele inscribed with Emperor Zhudi's story and the tale of his rebuilding of Mount Wudang. Purple Sky Hall, which was constructed on a platform, is the central hall, and enshrines the Emperor Zhenwu. There are 33 statues of Zhenwu, of which the central and largest one depicts him as emperor; the four medium-sized bronze figures on either side portray him as young, in middle age, and in old age; 28 smaller statues are arrayed along the eastern and western walls. The first floor of the Parents Hall enshrines the Holy Parents of the Emperor, while the second enshrines the Jade Emperor and the Mother of the Big Dipper.

Great Harmony Palace was established in 1416. The central hall enshrines a golden statue of the Emperor, with the Eight Heavenly Masters of the Thunder Ministry on either side. Other buildings include a Worship Hall, Bell and Drum Tower, Chanting Hall, Three-Element Gods Hall, and a theater. On Little Lotus Peak opposite is the so-called Transferred Hall, in which is a miniature bronze temple on a stone altar, donated in 1307 by followers from Hubei, Henan, and Zhejiang; it was moved from Golden Roof Palace on the order of Emperor Zhudi, who thought it too small to be on the highest peak, hence the hall's name.

The Gold Roof Palace is the atop Heaven's Pillar Peak, the mountain's tallest. It is an all bronze hall built upon a granite terrace. It is 5.54 meters high, 4.4 meters long, and 3.15 meters wide, and was constructed in 1416 using 21 tons of bronze and 30 kilograms of gold. The inner statues of the Emperor, Divine Generals of Water and Fire, and male and female escorts, as well as all the decorative ware are made of gold-plated bronze.

Other sacred Daoist sites too important to ignore are: the Temple of the Wall and Moat in Shanghai, Three Elements Palace in Guangzhou, Mount Luofu in Guangdong, Mount Lu in Jiangxi, Great Pure Palace in Shenyang, Obscure Mystery Temple in Suzhou, Master Lao's Cave in Chongqing, Mount Lao in Qingdao, Mount Qian in Liaoning, Black Goat Palace in Chengdu, Eight Immortals Palace in Xi'an, and Mount Mian in Shanxi. All are immense store-houses of Chinese history and culture, whose mystical beauty continues to attract those desiring peace and unity with nature.

CHAPTER 6

IMPORTANT DAOIST SCRIPTURES AND THE COMPILATION OF THE DAOIST CANON

THE DEVELOPMENT OF DAOIST SCRIPTURES

Daoist scriptures are numerous and voluminous because Daoism has drawn from many ancient folk beliefs and philosophical systems. The most important sources are ancient treatises on immortal doctrines, *yin-yang* and five-elements theories; astrology, medicine, and the numerology of the school of logicians; works on military strategy; and the philosophical schools of Moism and Legalism of the Spring and Autumn and Warring States periods. There also existed many "celestial books" or "sacred books" on millennialism which spread among the masses during the 2nd century, in the formative stages of religious Daoism, as well as books written by followers and scholars corresponding to the demands of feudal society, and in response to Confucian and Buddhist influence in later times. The subjects ranged from history to philosophy to ethics, astronomy, medicine, metallurgy, calendar, aesthetics, theology, anthropology, cultivation of the body, charms, liturgies, and commandments. The extant *Daoist Canon* (*Dao Zang*), compiled during the reigns of the two emperors Zhengtong and Wanli of the Ming Dynasty, has 5485 scrolls in total, making it the only religious canon that can compare in extent with the Buddhist *Tripitaka*.

Similar to Daoist religious development, the compilation and canonization of Daoist books has been a long historical process. In the 2nd century, the books that were canonized by the earliest Daoist religious sects, the Five Bushels Sect and the Supreme Peace Sect, were the *Book of Supreme Peace,* and the *Daode Jing* and its commentaries, such as those of Xiang'er and Heshanggong. Since its first appearance, the *Book of Supreme Peace* has had many different names and versions, while the *Daode Jing* has been the text most widely propagated and explicated by Daoist masters and their followers from varying perspectives. Among the commentaries available today, that of Heshanggong (literally, the "Revered Old Man by the River"), was the first to explain the *Daode Jing* from the perspective of Huang-Lao Daoism. This commentary, which is commonly regarded as a work edited during the middle of the Later Han dynasty, formulated the theory of "identification of body and state," which proposed that the principles of cultivation of personal health and state management are identical in that both require purity, reduction of desire, and accomplishment by means of *wu wei.*

The number of Daoist scriptures increased with the development and spread of Daoism. During the Eastern Jin dynasty, Gehong listed a catalogue of 1299 scrolls of Daoist books in the "Further Reading" chapter of his *The Philosopher Who Embraces Simplicity.* With the rapid spread of the Zhengyi Sect, Daoist charms and liturgies had been further elaborated on, resulting in the production of a many classics. These works come from three major traditions: Shangqing, Lingbao, and Sanhuang. The Shangqing tradition honored its founder, Madam Wei, who ascended on the Southern Sacred Mountain. Its exponents, among whom were Yangxi and Xumi, composed many works in Madam Wei's name, the most important of which is the *Supreme Pure Insight into the True Classics*. The Lingbao tradition claimed that its earliest scripture had been found in a stone city by Helu, King of the State of Wu during the Warring States Period. The Supreme Master Lao had sent Three Sage-Perfect Men to grant many scriptures to Gexuan, who had practiced cultivation at Tiantai Mountain. The Lingbao tradition continued to amass scriptures as well.

The Sanhuang tradition honored Baoliang, father-in-law of Gehong, as its founder. There are different stories concerning the origin of these scriptures: one held that they were found in a stone house on the central sacred mountain by Baoliang in 292 AD; the other is that they were granted to Baoliang by his teacher, Zuo Yuanfang, or Zhengying, an occult practitioner of the Later Han dynasty. The majority of the contents of the Sanhuang scriptures concern rituals of exorcism, charms, talismans, and cultivation methods based of concentration on deities. All of the scriptures of these three traditions converged into the *Daoist Canon*.

COMPILATIONS OF THE DAOIST CANON

The compilation of the *Daoist Canon* began during the Tang dynasty, when Daoism had its first prosperous period. Under the powerful patronage of emperors of the Li family, the collection and compilation of Daoist scriptures reached new heights. Tang Emperor Xuanzong ordered Shi Chongxuan and another 40 scholars to compile a complete set of Daoist scriptures during his Kaiyuan era (713–741). Using this work of 113 scrolls as a base, he sent researchers into provinces to bring back more Daoist texts. These were then compiled into the first *Daoist Canon*, the *Exquisite Compendium of Three Insights*. "Insight" is a translation of the Chinese *dong*, which many Western scholars translate as "grottoes," because the basic meaning of *dong* is "cave" or "grotto." However, in this sense it is equivalent to *tong*, which means "to communicate." Thus the "three insights" (*sandong*) are actually three ways of communicating with deities, in other words, three insights into the supernatural. These texts are all believed to be revelations from deities. The total number of scrolls recorded was 3744, which were classified according to their contents into three canons, each with 36 subdivisions: *Insights into the Perfect,* with 12 subdivisions; *Insights into the Mysterious,* with 12 subdivisions; and *Insights into the Sacred,* with 12 subdivisions. It was titled the *Daoist Canon of Kaiyuan* because it was printed in the Kaiyuan era.

The Song dynasty is the second period of the expansion and promotion of Daoism. Daoist canons were compiled on six occasions during the Song: 1) In the early years of the Song dynasty, Emperor Taizong ordered officials of all local governments to

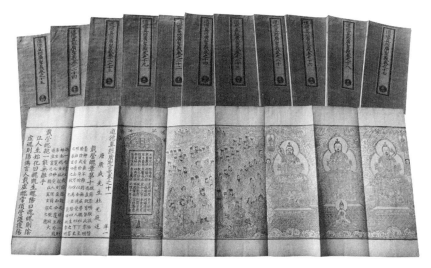

MING DYNASTY WOODBLOCK-PRINTED EDITION OF THE *DAOIST CANON* AT WHITE CLOUD TEMPLE, BEIJING.

search for Daoist texts. More than 7000 scrolls were collected. After making many amendments, duplicates were expunged, resulting in a compilation of 3737 scrolls. 2) In 1008, a further supplement reached 4359 total scrolls. 3) In 1012, this work was again supplemented to become the *Precious Canon of the Celestial Palace of the Great Song*, in 4565 scrolls. 4) For the convenience of the emperor's reading, chief editor Zhang Junfang extracted 122 scrolls from the more than 700 designated as the most important classics in the *Great Song* compilation, resulting in the *Yunji Qiqian* (literally, *Cloud Chests with Seven Labels*) in fact meaning a complete Daoist canon, but popularly referred to as the *Small Daoist Canon*. 5) During the reign of Emperor Song Huizong, who as an ardent believer in Daoism, the *Daoist Canon* was re-compiled twice; the

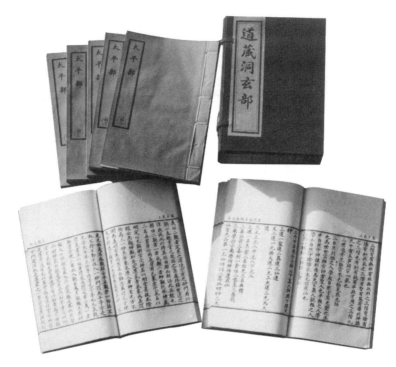

REPRINT OF A *DAOIST CANON* FROM THE EARLY YEARS OF THE PEOPLES' REPUBLIC, AT WHITE CLOUD TEMPLE, BEIJING.

later edition was the *Daoist Canon of Wanshou,* which contained 5481 scrolls. 6) In 1179 a compilation was once again undertaken by the rulers of the Southern Song dynasty to reconstruct the canon scattered in warring northern China; this resulted in a work with the same number of scrolls as that of the *Wanshou Canon.*

In the meantime, Emperor Zhangzong of the Jin Dynasty, who ruled in North China, ordered Daoists to supplement the *Wanshou Canon.* The fruit of their efforts was the *Precious Xuandu Canon of Great Jin* (Xuandu is the name of a Daoist temple), which totaled

6455 scrolls. The new edition of the *Xuandu Canon,* compiled in 1244 during the Yuan Dynasty, contained 7800 scrolls and was supplemented with scriptures of the Quanzhen sect that was in ascendancy at that time.

These editions of the *Daoist Canon* have mostly been lost; only a few remnant scrolls survive. The available editions today are the *Zhentong Daoist Canon* and *Wanli Supplementary Daoist Canon.* These are fruits of projects undertaken under Ming rulers Yingzong in the 15th century and Shenzong in the 17th century. The total of the two editions is 5485 scrolls.

The scriptures were arranged in *Three Insights* or *Three Primary Canons, Four Secondary Canons,* and *Twelve Accessory Canons.* The so-called *Three Insights* or *Three Primary Canons* followed the classification system of past editions. All scriptures believed to be granted by the Heavenly Sage of the Pre-existence (Yuanshi Tianzun) were included in *Insights into the Perfect,* of which most were from the Lingbao tradition; all scriptures that were believed to be bestowed by Supreme Master of Dao (Heavenly Sage of the Lingbao) were classified as *Insights into the Mysterious,* of which most were from the Lingbao tradition; all scriptures that were believed to be granted by Supreme Master of Lao were classified as *Insights into the Sacred,* of which most were from the Sanhuang tradition. The so-called *Four Secondary Canons* include *Great Purity, Great Peace, Great Mystery,* and *Zhengyi* canons. All books in these canons were expository and complementary to one or more of the *Three Insights. Great Purity* texts were expository and complementary to *Insights into the Perfect; Great Peace* texts to *Insights into the*

Mysterious; Great Mystery texts to *Insights into the Sacred;* and *Zhengyi* to all *Three Insights. Twelve Accessory Canons* were miscellaneous scriptures that could not be classified into the *Three Insights* or the *Four Secondary Canons;* they were grouped as: Texts, Sacred Talismans, Jade Secrets, Sacred Charts, Theogonies, Commandments, Liturgies, Cultivation Methods, Esoteric Skills, Biographies, Hymns, and Sacred Memorials

In 1900, when Western forces invaded Beijing, the wooden printing blocks of the *Zhentong Daoist Canon* and the *Wanli Supplementary Daoist Canon* were burned. Only one set of the *Daoist Canon* from the Ming was kept preserved, at the White Cloud Temple. From 1923 to 1936, in order to rescue this cultural heritage, Zhao Erxun and other important scholars initiated a program of reprinting these texts. Using the Daoist Canon of White Cloud Temple as the source, they engaged Hanfenlou Bookstore in Shanghai to reprint 350 sets, each with 1120 volumes. These copies were called the Hanfenlou edition, which is the major version of the *Daoist Canon* available today. The familiar classics such as *Daode Jing, Zhuangzi, Book of Divine Deliverance, Classic of Pure Quiet,* and *Book of the Intuitive Enlightenment,* are all included in this collection.

Although there was no new compilation of the *Daoist Canon* undertaken in Qing dynasty, some important reference works were published, including the *Compilation of Important Books in the Daoist Canon,* the *Contents of the Compilation of Important Books in the Daoist Canon,* and the *Basic Index of Compilation of Important Books in the Daoist Canon.* The earliest edition of the *Compilation of*

Important Books in the Daoist Canon was completed by abstracting 173 books from the Daoist Canon of the Ming during the Jiaqing era (1796–1820). This collection was gradually supplemented, reaching 287 volumes in 1906. Since none of the 114 books which were added were included in the Ming dynasty *Daoist Canon,* they naturally became important materials for the study of Daoism during the Ming and Qing dynasties.

Another important event during the Qing dynasty was the discovery at the beginning of the 20th century by a Daoist monk named Wang Yuanlu of ancient scrolls in cave number17 at Mogao Caves at Dunhuang, in western China. Some long-lost Daoist classics were found among these scrolls, which are now called the Dunhuang Daoist Scriptures. These books, numbering 496 items, are hand-written, and date from the 6th to the 10th century, mostly from the reigns of Gaozong and Xuanzong of the Tang dynasty. Most of them are fragmentary, yet they remain important relics of great historical value for Daoist studies, and are crucial for both supplementing and collating the *Daoist Canon* of the Ming dynasty. Unfortunately, as a result of political corruption during the Qing dynasty, these scrolls were stolen from China, a first large batch by the British explorer Aurel Stein in 1907, and subsequently more scrolls by a Frenchman, Paul Pelliot, then a Russian, Pyotr Koslov, and finally a Japanese, Zuicho Tachibana. After the establishment of People's Republic of China, through the joint efforts of the Chinese government and overseas friends, a small number of the priceless Dunhuang scrolls have been brought back to their homeland and preserved.

COMPILATIONS OF
DAOIST CANONS IN THE PRC

After the establishment of the People's Republic of China in 1949, and especially since the implementation of reform policies in the 1980s, independence and prosperity have brought about a national cultural flourishing. In 1981, the World Religions Institute of the Chinese Academy of Social Sciences began to organize scholars to compile a *Synopses of the Daoist Canon,* which was subsequently published in 1991. Under editor-in-chief Ren Jiyu, a noted scholar of religious studies in contemporary China, this book included all entries of the 1473 books in the *Daoist Canon.* Using the four-part structure of the imperial library collections, a team of scholars researched each book's author and time period, and introduced the contents of each, resulting in the four parts: "Resumes of Authors and Editors," "A New Classification Directory," "Contents of the Daoist Canon and its Supplements," and an "Index of Authors and Titles," constituting an excellent reference work for Daoist textual studies. In 1988, in order to satisfy increasing interest in studies of Chinese history, culture, philosophy, religion, medicine, and health care, the State Cultural Relic Publishing House, Shanghai Bookstore and Tianjin Ancient Works Publishing House reprinted the *Daoist Canon* of the Ming dynasty, in sets of 36 volumes.

In the 1990s, Bashu Publishing House in Sichuan invited Daoist scholars to compile the *Daoist Books Outside the Canon.* This project collected hundreds of Daoist works not included in the Ming dynasty canon, resulting in 26 volumes. Works selected were not arranged according to the traditional scheme, but rather classified into ten groups according to content: lost ancient texts, classics, tenets and decrees, cultivation of health, commandments, liturgies, biographies of immortals, records of temples and sacred places, literature and catalogues, and addendums. This reflected the modern development of Daoism, and greatly facilitated Daoist studies. All selected books were recorded as composed or produced before the establishment of the People's Republic.

Works included meet one of three criteria: 1) those extant prior to but not collected in the *Daoist Canon* of the Ming dynasty, such as the silk scrolls of Huang-Lao Daoism excavated at Mawangdui in Hunan in 1970s, which are few but quite valuable; 2) different versions of some works already collected in the Ming *Daoist Canon*, which are important for comparison; 3) works produced after the Ming *Daoist Canon*, by far the largest group in this compilation. All books except Mawangdui silk scrolls were reprinted by photo-offset, thus retaining their original appearance and enabling readers to glimpse rare or even unique copies, as well as texts from private collections. The range of works is extensive, including some books by non-Daoists, thus not only enriching the content of the *Daoist Canon,* but also mirroring the Daoist tendencies toward secularization and unification of the three major traditional Chinese ideologies. Some Confucians had always been fascinated with Daoist studies or Daoist cultivation, and wrote treatises on these subjects, as well as many works focusing on the differences among the three ideologies. Consequently the publication of *Daoist Books Outside the*

Canon was welcomed warmly by both Daoists as well as those engaged in Daoist studies in China and abroad.

In August 1996, the Chinese Taoist Association, the World Religions Institute of the Chinese Academy of Social Sciences, and Huaxia Publishing House jointly set up a Compilation Committee for rectifying, editing, and publishing the Chinese *Daoist Canon*. This project was listed among the important programs of the Ninth and Tenth Five-Year Plan of the National Publication Project. This edition of the *Daoist Canon* covers all books from the Ming edition and the most important Daoist books outside the Ming edition; all collected books were arranged according to four basic categories: primary scriptures, secondary scriptures, commandments, and Daoist history. All texts were emended, punctuated, typed, composed, and printed with modern techniques and the highest academic standards. All 49 volumes of this collection were published in 2003.

CHAPTER 7

THE CHINA TAOIST ASSOCIATION

Since the 15th and 16th centuries, China's three traditional belief systems of Confucianism, Buddhism, and Daoism have become more deeply integrated. At the beginning of its long history, Daoism followed two general trends: the first was the pursuit of longevity by emperors, nobles, and scholars; the second engaged in the various activities of folk cults. Although many important Daoist thinkers have reconstructed its ideological history, the social influence of Daoist organizations as an independent system has weakened in recent times. For example, both Mount Emei in Sichuan and Mount Heng in Hunan were historically Daoist sacred mountains and the site of numerous Daoist temples, but these have been overshadowed by Buddhist structures and trappings. In the 19th century China became reduced to a semi-colonial and semi-feudal country, in large part controlled by powerful Western countries. Daoism, along with Chinese culture in general, was greatly weakened. Most Daoist temples were destroyed or fell into ruin due to the fighting and chaotic conditions; Daoist organizations were cut off from normal social and financial support, and slowly withered; most Daoist clerics of those times were so poorly educated, they were unable to study their own tradition. However, the social and cultural foundation of Daoism has been preserved in traditional culture and folk customs.

The Establishment of CTA
and its Early Activities

Since 1949, when the People's Republic of China was established, the Chinese Communist Party and Chinese government have implemented a policy of religious tolerance. The Constitution of China clearly stipulates that citizens have the freedom to believe or not believe in religions, that differences in religious belief should not result in any differences in either rights or obligations, and that all religions are legally equal.

Although Daoism has fewer clerics and temples than the other major religions, it has the same right of religious freedom, and is

White Cloud Temple in Beijing is the founding temple of the Dragon Gate Sect of Daoism and the location of the headquarters and offices of the China Taoist Association (CTA).

protected by the law. In 1956, after Buddhism and Islam first established their national associations, some Daoist notables proposed a Chinese Taoist Association (abbreviated CTA, based on the pre-*pinyin* spelling of Daoism), and Daoists throughout China responded. In April 1956, the First National Conference of Daoist Representatives was held in Beijing. At that time they announced the establishment of CTA and elected a governing council composed of members from both the Zhengyi and Quanzhen denominations, among whom Yue Chongdai, the Abbot of the Supreme Pure Palace (Taiqing Gong) in Shenyang and the 26th generation Liturgy Master of the Dragon Gate Sect, was appointed president. They decided that the association's offices would be established at the White Cloud Temple in Beijing.

The CTA is the first national interdenominational organization in Daoist history. Its current institutions, which are responsible for coordination of Daoist affairs, include the Ecclesiastic Affairs Office, Liaison Office, Office of Research, and Administrative Office.

The activities of CTA were forced to cease during the Cultural Revolution (1966–1976). Since the end of that period, the CTA has continued to hold its National Representative Conference every five years, and its Standing Council has held elections six times. In addition, there are now more than 50 local Daoist Associations throughout China.

In the 1950s and 1960s the biggest challenge for Daoism in China was to restore and revive its debilitated state. The CTA organized the repair of damaged temples and the collection of scriptures under government support. It also encouraged Daoists to study culture, politics, and religious teachings. The second president, also a noted Daoist scholar, Chen Yingning, chaired the drafting of the "Working Plan Concerning Daoist Research and the Intellectual Training of Clerics," and directed Daoists and scholars to collect and compile Daoist books, rubbings, papers, and pictures in order to write a *History of China Daoism*. The detailed *Synopses of Daoist Canon* this group produced exceeds 300,000 Chinese characters; they completed as well the first edition of *Memorabilia of Daoism in Past Dynasties* and final editions of several books, among which this brief introduction to Daoism is the first systemic introduction to Daoism in modern times. They also regularly publish the only Daoist magazine, *Chinese Taoism*.

In September, 1962, the CTA initiated clerical training classes for Chinese Daoists. There were two kinds of programs: senior training, which is aimed at Daoist researchers, and clerical training, whose purpose is to educate the administrative and liturgical staff. The curricula can be divided into three groups: 1) basic Daoist subjects, which include tenets, denominational history, major classics, commandments, and liturgy; 2) basic cultural knowledge, which includes the history of Daoism, biographies of Daoist historical figures, and the philosophy of Laozi, Zhuangzi, and other schools; and 3) the subjects related to Daoist cultivation, which include *qigong,* medicine, as well as inner and outer alchemy. The length of training is five years. The graduates from the classes numbered more than thirty persons, all of who have become the cadre staff of Daoist institutions throughout China. These classes were stopped during Cultural Revolution.

THE LIBRARY OF QINCHIYING TEMPLE IN THE NEW DISTRICT OF PUDONG ISLAND, SHANGHAI.

THE ACTIVITIES OF DAOISM
IN THE ERA OF CHINESE REFORMATION

Since the end of the Cultural Revolution, Chinese Daoism has been growing more prosperous with the rapid development of the economy and society in general, as well as policies of religious freedom.

The CTA has played a role as mediator between the government and Daoists. Several years after resuming its work following the end of the Cultural Revolution, the CTA held a Third National Representative Conference, in May of 1980, at which time it modified its constitution and elected a new council and president. It took over ten years to clarify the mistaken religious policies of the Cultural Revolution, establish just new ones, redress mishandled cases, and hand back and repair occupied or closed temples.

Since then, many Daoist temples have been renovated and reopened, and other buildings newly constructed Many young people have converted to the religion and become monks (see the Introduction). However, it is impossible to calculate the number of ordinary believers of Daoism because there is no formal initiation ritual for lay adherents. Research published in *Shanghai Daoism* (the first issue of 2003) revealed that, among the templegoers of the nine Daoist temples in Shanghai, 32% were men and 68% women; 46% were between 30 and 60 years of age, while 45% above age 60; 50% were primary school graduates and 41% middle school graduates; more than half had believed in Daoism for over 15 years, while one third had believed for 8 to 15 years, and more than half believed in two religions, usually Daoism and Buddhism.

ZHANG JIYU, VICE PRESIDENT OF THE CHINA TAOIST ASSOCIATION, TALKS WITH A BRITISH DAOIST DURING THE CONFERENCE OF WORLD RELIGIONS AND DEVELOPMENT, HELD IN THE UNITED KINGDOM.

The purposes of individual participation in temple activities were found to be: 42% for petitioning for safety, success in one's career, or better health; 20% for self cultivation; and a very limited percentage for an abundant harvest, happy marriage, or future off-spring. The hierarchy of these concerns mirrors China's change from a chiefly agrarian society to a modern industrial power.

The rapid development of this socialist country has also inspired the enthusiasm of Daoists. The leaders of Chinese Daoism agree that, as the only indigenous Chinese religion, Daoism has unique cultural resources and profound roots in folk culture, and can play a positive role both in China and in the world. With the implementation of policies of religious freedom in China, Daoism can play an important part in promoting social stability by guiding people to assume proper living values and cultivate harmonious spiritual states. Daoism can show people how to maintain an independent morality and spirituality while sailing in the currents of modern social development; how to abide by natural rules to maintain a sustainable harmony between nature and society; how to balance the economic development of the world with the general welfare and the desires of individual human beings; how to refrain from greed and extravagance while still enjoying a basic material satisfaction; and how to cultivate oneself effectively by integrating personal salvation internally with altruism externally, using a method that combines patriotism with piety.

CTA MEMBERS DONATE FUNDS FOR AID TO FLOOD VICTIMS, 1998.

THE *SHOULU* RITUALS OF ZHENGYI DAOISM.

Since 1978, under the coordination and promotion of Daoist associations at all levels, Chinese Daoist temples have done much work for social welfare, including private almsgiving, public donations, and tree planting. In 1993, the CTA held the first convention to commend model individuals and groups with respect to both patriotism and religious piety, in which 53 groups and 159 persons received honors. In the summer of 1998, when the Yangtze River, Songhua River, and Nen River all flooded, the Chinese Daoist Association donated the equivalent of $700,000 in disaster relief funds. Daoists have won respect and trust from the people; in 2003 there were five Daoist priests elected as national political consultants and three as national people's representatives, two of whom hold standing membership in both organizations.

DISCIPLES PERFORM THE COMMANDMENT RITES BY FOLLOWING THE INSTRUCTING MASTER AT THE FIRST *CHUANJIE* CEREMONY OF THE PRC, AT WHITE CLOUD TEMPLE, BEIJING, 1989.

The CTA has reinstated Daoist traditional systems and rituals that had not been practiced in decades. The CTA has instituted and issued rules concerning temple affairs and Daoist clerics, and facilitated the administration of Daoist affairs.

The Quanzhen and Zhengyi sects have their own specific succession systems and liturgies; those of Quanzhen are called *chuanjie* (literally, "to pass down commandments"),while those of Zhengyi are called *shoulu* (literally, "to bestow the sacred registry"). The system of *chuanjie* in Quanzhen Daoism, founded by Qiu Chuji in the 13th century, has a history of over 700 years; and that of *shoulu* in Zhengyi Daoism, founded by Zhang Daoling in the 2nd century, has a history of over 1800 years. The *shoulu* assemblies were often held on the days before Triplet Days, because these are occasions when the Three Elements Gods inspect human deeds and determine blessings and punishments accordingly.

It subsequently became a custom for the Celestial Masters to descend to altars to bestow sacred registries in the Mansion on Mount Dragon and Tiger on the Triplet Days. *Lu* is an entry in the registry book of deities from all directions, but also the certificate to summon divine generals to execute Daoist orders. Zhengyi Daoists believe that only after having been bestowed with *lu* can they ascend to the Heavenly Court and get divine positions. Only

DISCIPLES FOLLOWING THE RIGHTS IN THE *CHUANJIE* CEREMONY AT FIVE DRAGON PALACE ON MOUNT QIAN LIAONING.

those who have divine positions can make their memorials to Heaven heard or seen in ceremonies, and thereby command divine soldiers or generals.

Shoulu ceremonies are presided over by the Three Masters, of Proselytism, Inspection, and Recommendation. Since the 24th generation, the Celestial Master was authorized by Emperor Zhengzong of the Northern Song (r. 997–1022) to set up a *shoulu* court in the capital city, and in these ceremonies the Proselytizing Master has always been played by the Celestial Masters themselves.

In the Daoist tradition, *chuanjie* and *shoulu* are not only ordination ceremonies which call for participants' belief in Dao and their commitment to priesthood, but also educational ceremonies to regulate the words and deeds of priests. In modern times, war and chaotic conditions halted the practice of these rituals for decades. Although the White Cloud Temple in Beijing was the central place for *chuanjie,* no such ceremony had been held since the 1920s.

It was the ardent desire of Daoists, and a reflection of the times as well, that these rituals of passage be resumed. In November 1988, it was decided to hold a *chuanjie* ceremony at

STUDENTS BROWSING IN THE LIBRARY OF THE CHINA TAOIST COLLEGE, BEIJING.

NUNS DISCUSS DAOIST TEXTS.

White Cloud Temple in Beijing on the Second Meeting of the Fourth Session Council of the CTA. On the 2nd day of the 12th month of 1989, the long absent rituals were reinstituted at White Cloud Temple in a *chuanjie* ceremony that lasted for twenty days. The Chair Master was Wang Lixian, the 22nd Abbot of White Cloud Temple in Beijing; the 17 Auxiliary Masters came from other important Quanzhen temples. In all, 45 Quanzhen monks and 30 nuns participated, among whom the oldest was 75 years old and the youngest, 21.

During these ceremonies, drum and bell sounded together in the morning; the participant monks and nuns rose early, dressed in yellow robes and, holding scriptures in hands, chanted along with presiding masters. This took place three times each day, morning, noon, and afternoon. After the participants were instructed in all important rites and classics, they were bestowed with Primary, Secondary, and Celestial Commandments, respectively, along with Commandment Certificates, according to their levels. These serve as their religious identity cards, certifying what level of rites, commandments, and hence ordination rank they had received.

In November 1995, the CTA held a second *chuanjie* assembly on Mount Qingcheng in Sichuan, in which 546 Quanzhen monks and 166 nuns from across the country participated. The oldest

STUDENTS ATTEND A LECTURE AT THE SHANGHAI DAOIST COLLEGE.

among them was 120 years old, the youngest, 21. The president of the CTA and the 23rd generation succession master, Fu Yuantian, presided over the ceremonies. What was unique this occasion was that there were several lectures on cultivation methods for nuns, moral practices, and master-student relationships. Some Daoist scholars and artists were also invited to observe the ceremonies.

The third *chuanjie* assembly was held on Mount Qian, Liaoning Province, in August 2002. About 400 Quanzhen monks and nuns participated this event, including some from Hong Kong, Taiwan, Malaysia, and Singapore; 200 participants received complete ordinations and 200 more received incomplete ordinations.

The situation of Zhengyi priests is quite different from that of Quanzhen clerics in that they live very much like ordinary people. Thus the importance of ordination ceremony to Zhengyi priests is not limited to the recognition of their priesthood, but the effort to elevate their awareness of a responsibility for preaching and promoting salvation. The CTA questioned some Zhengyi priests, held colloquia, and compiled and issued some documents on *shoulu*.

In October 1991, the CTA re-instituted *shoulu* ceremonies on Mount Dragon and Tiger for 36 Zhengyi priests from Taiwan, Singapore, and Malaysia.

From September 5th to 7th, 1995, the CTA held the first *shoulu* ceremonies for Zhengyi priests in mainland China on Mount Dragon and Tiger. More than 190 persons attended the rites, among whom the oldest was 70 years old and the youngest was less than 20. A senior priest from Mount Dragon and Tiger assumed the role of Proselytizing Master. After performing a series of rites prescribed by traditional regulations, all the participants succeeded in obtaining their divine positions.

On the Lower Principles Day in November 2002, the Celestial Master's Mansion held master-disciple recognition ceremonies for more than 60 Daoists from Taiwan, Hong Kong, Singapore, and Indonesia.

In the meantime, in 1992, in order to purify and conserve the spiritual tradition of Daoism, reform the confusing situation between Daoism and folk religions, and between Daoist clerics and wizards, the CTA issued "Administrative Measures on Daoist Temples" and "Trial Measures on the Administration of Zhengyi Priests." The former document prescribes that all Daoist temples must establish a Democratic Management Committee through election among the resident clerics. This committee then takes responsibility for internal affairs. All activities held in any temple must conform to Daoist traditional norms, abide by the constitution and laws of the country, and may not engage in any superstitious feudal activity in the name of Daoism. The financial affairs, cultural relics protection, recruitment, external relationships, and accommodation for visiting clerics must be executed according to appropriate regulations.

STUDENTS ATTEND A COMPUTER CLASS AT THE CHINA TAOIST COLLEGE.

The latter document was issued to protect legal rights and interests of Zhengyi priests, and administrate their activities according to standard rules. It demands that all Zhengyi priests must be patriotic, law-abiding, and formally abide by the Three Jewels of Dao, Scriptures, and Masters; they must have a master-disciple lineage, be able to recite the *Precious Instructions of Founder Masters* and the *Classic of Morning and Evening Monastic Lessons*, perform the daily rites of the Zhengyi denomination, abide by the norms of the words and deeds of a priest, and pass an examination, thereby receiving the recognition of Daoist organizations. The CTA uniformly grants the Certificate of Daoist Priest to qualified Zhengyi applicants. They must accept the administration of the local Daoist temple or asso-

A VARIETY OF PUBLICATIONS OF THE CHINA TAOIST ASSOCIATION.

ciation, and hold ceremonies in registered temples. If they hold a ceremony in a follower's house, as traditional custom requires, they must have the agreement of the local Daoist temple or association, and avoid disturbing the social, living, or productive orders. These policies have played positive roles in promoting the preservation and development of the Daoist tradition.

The CTA has founded the first Daoist school in history to train new gen-erations of Daoist clerics. Daoism has been passed down through master-disciple lines since it came into being. Although there were some knowledgeable masters who gave special seminars during their spiritual wanderings, these courses were not consistent and

the curricula were not systematic. After its foundation in 1957, the
CTA held one Daoist cleric training program in 1962, and six during the 1980s, with 206 graduates in total, most of whom have
become the major functionaries in Daoist temples or associations
across the country today.

In May 1990, the CTA founded the China Taoist College (CTC)
at White Cloud Temple in Beijing, based on these earlier training
programs. The mission of the CTC is to educate young Daoists to
have a certain level of Daoist knowledge and accomplishment, to
be both patriotic and pious, to volunteer to serve in the Daoist
vocation, and to carry on and develop Daoist tradition and culture.

Daoist monks from the UK, Germany, and Korea at a meeting hosted by the CTA.

SCENE FROM THE SYMPOSIUM ON "DAOIST THOUGHT AND SOCIAL PROGRESS IN CHINA," HOSTED BY THE CTA AND THE SHANGHAI DAOIST ASSOCIATION, 1962.

There are two kinds of classes, specialized classes and general classes. The former are two-year classes to train administrators for temples. Applicants should have at least two years of experience as Daoist clerics, have the recommendation of a local Daoist temple or association, and the approval from their families. They must also pass an entrance examination. The latter are also two-year classes, for which the applicants are qualified graduates from the former school or from local Daoist schools.

The main courses of the college are Daoist history, teachings, liturgies, commandments, introduction to Daoist classics, Daoist liturgical music, catalogue of the Daoist pantheon, Daoist cultivation methods, Daoist sculpture and pottery, temple management, foreign language study, calligraphy, Chinese history and geography,

A Daoist delegation from Taiwan during a visit to White Cloud Temple, Beijing.

world history and geography, and legal knowledge. The teachers are reputable Daoist masters and accomplished scholars. The CTC has recruited about 200 students since its foundation, and has become the chief place to train middle- to high-level Daoist clerics.

Additionally, the CTC has hosted some temporary programs. In May 1997, it held a seminar for 27 principals of Daoist temples from 20 provinces, among whom 17 were male and 10 were female, 24 were of the Quanzhen sect, and 3 were of the Zhengyi sect. From 1998 to 2001, it held a class for 22 Zhengyi priests in Shanghai, all of whom were qualified graduates from the Shanghai Daoist College.

There are also local schools or seminars hosted by Daoist associations of various levels, such as those of Shanghai, Sichuan, Wuhan, Mount Mao, Suzhou, Shaanxi. and Lanzhou. Most temples have systems or programs of training and studies. Thus the CTA has formed a pyramid structure for Daoist education, with the CTC at the apex.

The CTA has researched Daoist doctrines and history in order to preserve and promote Daoist culture. In May 1980, after the CTA had just reassumed functioning, it made a decision to take studies on Daoism as its key work. By 1986, the Study Office of CTA had published 16 issues of the *CTA Journal*, the predecessor to *China Taoism* magazine, which has been a periodical since 1987. It is now a bimonthly journal available in China and abroad with a distribution of more than

A REPRESENTATIVE OF THE CTA ACCEPTING MEMORIAL GIFTS AT THE CONSECRATION CEREMONIES OF THE THREE PURE ONES HALL. MOUNT LOTUS, MALAYSIA.

8,000 copies. It is welcomed by readers who want to learn about Daoist history, doctrines, and studies, as well as CTA proceedings. It has the fourth largest overseas circulation among Chinese social science periodicals. There are also other Daoist magazines issued by some local Daoist associations, such as *Shanghai Daoism, Sanqin Daoism,* and *Fujian Daoism.*

The CTA has also published some books on Daoism and numerous Daoist scriptures, altogether accounting for about 1,154,000 copies of more than 120 titles; among the most important of these are the *Great Dictionary of Daoism, Album for Chinese Daoism, An Introduction to Daoism, Daoism and Health Cultivation, Commentary on the Daode Jing, Collection of Daoist Calligraphy and Paintings* and the *Classic of Morning and Evening Monastic Lessons.*

THE VICE PRESIDENT OF THE HONG KONG TAOIST ASSOCIATION PRESENTING A GIFT TO AN OFFICIAL OF THE RELIGIOUS AFFAIRS BUREAU DURING A DAOIST FESTIVAL IN HONG KONG.

A RELIGIOUS DELEGATION FROM TAIWAN DURING A VISIT TO WHITE CLOUD TEMPLE, BEIJING.

In order to promote Daoist studies by ecclesiastic and scholastic groups, both domestic and overseas, the CTA set up the Daoist Culture Institute (TCI) in 1989, through which the CTA has broadened the field of Daoist studies through publishing activities and hosting symposiums. In autumn 1992, the TCI, Xi'an Daoist Association, and Eight Immortals Palace in Xi'an hosted jointly a Xi'an Daoist Culture Symposium, which 55 representatives attended from 12 Chinese provinces, as well as from Japan and France; the TCI and Mount Wudang Daoist Association jointly held symposiums twice, in 1993 and 1994, on Mount Wudang, in

THE SHANGHAI DAOIST ASSOCIATION PRAYS FOR WORLD PEACE.

which 40 representatives from China, Japan, Italy, and Korea participated and more than 30 theses were delivered.

The TCI and Immortal's Cave Temple on Mount Lu in Jiangxi Province held symposiums in 1998 and 1999. More than 100 representatives from mainland China, Hong Kong, and Taiwan participated and presented more than 100 papers on topics such as the status of Daoism, its role in Chinese traditional culture, modern values of Daoism, trends of Daoism in the new century, and the Daoist relationship to socialist construction. In August 2001, the TCI, along with the Daoist association of Jiangsu Province, Mount Mao, and Nanjing University, held a symposium on Mount Mao, the theme of which was "Prospects for Daoism in the 21st Century."

In November 2002, the TCI and the Shanghai Daoist Association held joint symposiums in Shanghai, the topic of which was Daoist thought and social progress in China, and nearly 100 representatives presented papers. Reverend Min Zhiting, the president of the CTA, stated in his speech that: "In order to carry on and develop Daoist teaching, we must understand that on the one hand, we have entered a new stage of building a generally prosperous society. Therefore Daoist doctrines have to adapt to the progress of a socialist society; and on the other hand, now that we are in a time of globalization, Daoist doctrines have to adapt to the progress of human civilization."

Reverend Zhang Jiyu, vice president of the CTA, observed that under the new historical conditions, all Daoists were concerned

A JAPANESE DELEGATION FROM THE WORLD RELIGIONS AND PEACE COMMITTEE VISITS THE CTA IN 1992.

THE FORMER PRESIDENT OF AUSTRIA DURING A VISIT TO WHITE CLOUD TEMPLE, BEIJING.

with how to play a more important role in social development. All participants agreed that Daoism emphasizes the unification of cultivating Dao and accumulating virtue, and deems that to fulfill social duties is an indispensable part of the doctrine of immortals; the basic tenets of Daoism are unchangeable, while the method of organization, contents of commandments, liturgies, and exorcisms can alter with the times.

These events have deepened the study and public understanding of Daoism, helped to broaden and intensify the influence of Daoism both at home and abroad, and produced many constructive proposals for a better and more peaceful world.

The CTA has developed friendship with Daoists in Hong Kong, Taiwan, Macao, and foreign countries, and actively participated in world affairs to promote peace and justice. The central government of China has continually sought to implement a policy of One China, Two Systems in its relations with Hong Kong, Macao, and Taiwan. Therefore the religious bodies and individuals in these three Chinese zones do not affiliate with each other, nor do they intervene with each other; instead they have mutual respect for one another. The intercourse between the CTA and Hong Kong Daoist circles began formally on the Middle Principles Day of 1985, when 35 Quanzhen Daoists from Zique Daoist Temple in Hong Kong visited White Cloud Temple in Beijing to pay homage to the founding temple, and to join in the celebrations.

THE FORMER CHANCELLOR OF GERMANY DURING A VISIT TO WHITE CLOUD TEMPLE, BEIJING.

In January 1986, Reverend Li Yuhang, president of the CTA, went to Mount Luofu in Guangdong Province to preside over the reopening and abbot inauguration celebration, on which occasion he encountered the vice president, Wu Yaodong, and chairman Lu Chongde of the Hong Kong Daoist Association, and the vice abbot Zhao Zhendong and Deng Guocai of the Yuen Yuen Institute in Hong Kong. They had friendly talks, thereby establishing formal links.

In October 1986, a delegation from the Hong Kong Daoist Association visited the CTA in Beijing and Mount Laoshan Daoist Association in Shandong, interviewed Zhao Puchu, vice president of Chinese Consultant Conference, and attended a dinner party

CTA PRESIDENT MIN ZHITING ATTENDING A DAOIST FESTIVAL AT MOUNT MIAN. SHANXI PROVINCE.

hosted by the Religious Affairs Bureau under the State Council. Since then intercourse and exchange among mainland Daoist bodies and those of Hong Kong and Macao have continued.

The intercourse among mainland Daoist groups and those of Taiwan started in 1988. Soon after reassuming work in 1980, the CTA published *A Letter to Daoist Friends in Taiwan,* lamenting the separation of mainland Daoists from their friends across the straits, extending invitations to them, and welcoming them to make pilgrimages to mainland temples, to exchange views on teachings, increase friendship, and contribute to the reunion of the nation.

In April 1988, a delegation of six headed by Long Jinlian, vice president of Fuyou Palace in Southern Taiwan, visited Eight Immortals Palace in Xi'an, Shaanxi Province, and requested the transfer of a replica of Lu Dongbin's statue to Taiwan, which was later consecrated there in a ceremony attended by by 50,000.

On August 2, 1988, a delegation of 26 pilgrims from Cisheng Palace in central Taiwan arrived at the Celestial Master's Mansion in Jiangxi Province to pay homage to the ancient temple. The two daughters and one nephew (Zhang Jintao, who is now the president of the Mansion) of the 36th generation Celestial Master Zhang Enfu received them. This delegation also entreated the temple to transfer two replicas of a statue of Zhang Daoling to Taiwan.

On August 8, 1989, a delegation of 15 persons from the Chinese Daoist Association in Taiwan, headed by its deputy secretary-general, Zhangsheng, visited the CTA and expressed their sincere wishes to enhance mutual friendship. Zhangsheng said: "No matter what happens, the intercourse among Daoists of Taiwan

GREAT PURITY PALACE, MOUNT LAO. SHANDONG PROVINCE.

and the mainland should not break off, because we have the same founder. Only by believing in Daoism and only by purity, calm, and non-artificial striving, can Chinese people lead happy lives."

One month later, a delegation from Gaoxiong Culture Institute and Taoyuan Mingsheng Daoist Monastery in Taiwan visited Master Lao's Cave in Chongqing, also expressing their wishes to enhance their relationship with mainland Daoist organizations. They noted that: "The roots of Daoism are on the mainland. It is our long cherished wish to return to the mainland and search for our roots. We will come back again for pilgrimages. Since the 1990s, the CTA has sent delegations to Taiwan to visit, give lectures, attend celebrations, hold ceremonies, and perform musical rituals.

The CTA also has had friendly intercourse with foreign Daoist organizations and scholastic institutes. In the 1950s and 60s, the noted Japanese Sinologist Fukunaga Mitsuji visited the CTA several times. In 1959, the eminent English Sinologist Joseph Needham visited White Cloud Temple and discussed alchemy with the famous scholar and president of the CTA, Chen Yingning.

In the 1980s, the CTA established friendly relations with other Daoist bodies around the world, among the most important of which are the French Daoist Association, the Singapore Daoist Association, the Institute of Oriental Culture of the University of Tokyo, the Three Pure Ones Temple in Malaysia, Zhongfu Daoist Temple in Arizona, Zigeng Temple in San Francisco, Taixuan Temple in Hawaii, the Taoist Taiqi Society, and Fung Loy Kok Institute of Taoism in Toronto.

By the beginning of this 21st century, the CTA had established friendly relationships with Daoist bodies, disciples, and scholars in about 30 countries, sent 27 delegations totaling 230 representatives to more than 10 countries, received 360 visiting groups numbering 35,000 people, include such notables as the former German Chancellor Kohl, and the American Henry Kissinger.

From the 17th to the 26th of September, 1993, the Daoist bodies of mainland China, Taiwan, and Hong Kong jointly held the Great Sacrificial Ceremony for Luotian (Luotian Dajiao) at the White Cloud Temple in Beijing, with the theme of "Praying for Peace for World, Country, and People." *Luotian* is the Daoist name for the empyrean, or highest Heaven, which surpass the Three Realms of Desire, Material, and Spirit. *Jiao* was the name of the

CTA VICE PRESIDENT XIE ZONGXIN AND DEPUTY SECRETARY-GENERAL ZHANG JIYU ATTENDING THE WORLD SUMMIT OF RELIGIONS AND CONSERVATION IN LONDON, 1994.

archaic sacrificial ceremony for Heaven, adopted by Daoism; *zhai* was the ceremony to appeal for Heaven's help. After the Sui Dynasty, *zhai* and *jiao* were used together to refer to all Daoist sacrificial ceremonies (sometimes shortened to simply *jiao*). Thus the Great Jiao (Dajiao) is a lengthy and important ceremony.

The present Luotian Dajiao was chaired by the president of the CTA, Fu Yuantian, and co-chaired by Hou Baoyuan, abbot of the Hong Kong Ching Chung Koon Temple; Gao Zhongxin, the abbot of Taipei Zhinan Palace; and Huang Xinyang, the deacon of White Cloud Temple in Beijing. Approximately 1200 statues of deities were installed in 10 shrines. The participants were White Cloud

Temple in Beijing, Hong Kong Qingsong Daoist Temple, Taipei Zhinan Palace, White Cloud Temple in Shanghai, Xuanmiao Temple in Suzhou, Baopu Daoist Temple in Hangzhou, Mount Wudang Daoist Association, Eight Immortals Palace in Xi'an, Mount Qingcheng Daoist Association, Sanyuan Palace in Guangzhou, Fung Ying Sin Koon in Hong Kong, Xingshan Daoist Temple in Hong Kong, and other Daoist temples in the United States, Canada, and Australia. The participants included foreign Daoists from Singapore, Malaysia, Japan, Korea, and France.

This Luotian Dajiao raised donations of approximately $125,000, all of which was subsequently donated to the Hope Project, the national education foundation for poor, generally rural, populations in China.

THE DAOIST ORCHESTRA OF SUZHOU DURING ITS PERFORMANCE TOUR.

MOUNT MIAN. SHANXI PROVINCE.

From May 21st to 30th, 2001, the CTA co-hosted a second Luotian Dajiao, in cooperation with the Shanxi Province Daoist Association and Jiexiu City Daoist Association in Shanxi Province, the theme of which was "Praying for World Peace, State Prosperity, National Reunion and the People's Happiness." Over 300 participants from Daoist associations based in Beijing, Shanghai, Jiangxi, Jiangsu, Sichuan, Hubei, Shanxi, Shaanxi, northeast China, Hong Kong, Macao, Taiwan, Singapore, and Korea installed 15 shrines.

From August 28 to 31, 2000, CTA president Min Zhiting and six other leaders of the five major Chinese religions participated in the Millennium World Peace Summit of Religious and Spiritual Leaders, held at the headquarters of the United Nations in New York City. There he offered a prayer in the name of Daoism at the opening celebration, in which he appealed for world peace and harmonious coexistence among all people akin to the closeness of family members. He also expressed wishes for China's reunification, peace, stability, and ethnic and religious harmony.

Min Zhiting further stated: "The ecological crisis of today is closely related to the egocentric values and the incessant exploitative thinking patterns of human beings; these have brought about great damage to nature. Hi-tech wars that might employ biochemical and nuclear weapons are especially threatening to both human life and our environment. Hence we Daoists advocate that: 1) only by changing our attitudes toward nature, recognizing the unity between man and nature, and following the way of nature can we realize sustainable development; 2) we must all respect life, control desires, refrain from killing animals and expand our benevolence to all creatures; 3) oppose all war and resolve disputes by negotiation, halt any actions damaging to the environment and live in natural ways." These views were widely appreciated and welcomed by people all over the world who love peace and nature.

From March 17th to 20th, 2003, the CTA launched and hosted the Grand Anniversary Celebration of Laozi's Birth, which conducted sacrificial ceremonies, memorial conferences, calligraphy and painting demonstrations, and Daoist concerts. The representatives came from various local Daoist organizations in Mainland China, Hong Kong, Macao, and Taiwan, as well as some Singapore and Malaysia. Reverend Min Zhiting said that the purpose of the memorial celebration of Laozi was to spread and carry on his doctrines of "respecting Dao and its Virtue," "imitating nature," "acting with benevolence and tolerance," "doing good and summoning good," and "being thrifty, not extravagant," and thereby promoting the development of Daoism. The art exhibition along with the concert enhanced the ceremony's cultural value. The concerts were performed by Daoist orchestras of White Cloud Temple in Beijing, Mount Mao in Jiangsu, Xuanmiao Temple in Suzhou, Mount Mian in Shanxi, the Hong Kong Penglai Daoist Temple, Gaoxiong Culture Institute, Wall and Moat God Temple in Singapore, and the Choir of Daode Jing of Dashibo Palace in Singapore.

CHAPTER 8

THE INFLUENCE OF DAOISM

Daoism has inherited much from early Chinese culture, and for centuries has interacted and often coalesced with the activities and doctrines of Confucianism and Buddhism, eventually coming to constitute one of the pillars of traditional Chinese culture. Thus the influence of Daoism surpasses greatly the modest circle of Daoist organizations, and has been an important factor in the molding of the Chinese character, behavior, thinking, and world views.

TANG DYNASTY BRUSH STROKE RENDERING OF THE CHARACTER *DAO*.

THE INFLUENCE OF DAOISM
ON CHINESE TRADITIONAL CULTURE

We can find traces of Daoism in the cosmology, ethics, and aesthetics of traditional Chinese philosophy. Laozi's cosmology, holding that one gave birth to two, two gave birth to three, and three gave birth to the ten thousand things, has always been the dominating metaphysical principle of the Chinese. The doctrines of correspondence between humans and the universe advocated by Daoism are still very much a part of the Chinese mentality. Many Chinese believe that the changes of the celestial bodies influence the social and personal trends, and, conversely, social and personal behavior can cause the fluctuations in the state of the universe.

CONSECRATING A STATUE AT FIVE DRAGON PALACE ON MOUNT QIAN. LIAONING PROVINCE.

Daoist moral norms of *wu wei,* purity, nature, the control of desire, thriftiness, yielding, benevolence, and harmony are important components of traditional morality. The Daoist pursuit of immortality in the real world has had great influence on Chinese aesthetics, reflected, for example, in such concepts as "returning to the origin," "embracing simplicity," and "wordless beauty." These kinds of ideas have been passed down through the centuries, and have become part of the Chinese spiritual identity.

DAOIST DISCIPLES OFFERING JOSS STICKS.

Daoism has also contributed greatly to Chinese medicine. Although the ultimate goal of Daoism is to identify with Dao and become immortal, the cultivation of the body and medicinal methods in pursuit of longevity have been considered necessary as preconditions. Hence Daoism has made use of medicinal lore and often led the way in Chinese medicine. Daoist ideas of "treatment before illness" and "consolidating life foundation" led Chinese medicine to put prevention at the forefront. The "vital energy" theory of Daoist cosmology is the basic principle of both Daoist cultivation and Chinese medicine. Some Daoist classics are also very important medical treatises, such as the *Classic of Internal Medicine*

THE GODS OF THE BIG DIPPER.

of the Yellow Emperor, the *Synopsis of Prescriptions of the Golden Chamber* and the *Collection of Commentaries on the Divine Farmer's Classic of Medicinal Herbs.* Many Daoist masters were also great doctors, such as Gehong, Tao Hongjin, and Sun Simiao.

Daoism has also been closely related to Chinese arts. First of all, the aesthetic values of Daoism, as referred to above, provide the intrinsic context of all Chinese arts; the celestial world and transcendent images are key components. The images of running or flying divine birds and animals fill the decorated spaces of excavated bronze ware from the 5th to 3rd century BCE. The work of Wang Yanshou, an artist of the Former Han dynasty, depicted immortals, fairy maidens, and red phoenixes, as well as Fuxi, the hero-ancestor who invented the eight trigrams (*bagua*) of the *Book of Changes* (*Yijing*), and Nuwa, the heroine-ancestor with the body of snake. After religious Daoism came into being in the second century CE, paintings of immortal stories and Daoist teachings played a greater part in Chinese art. Some of these works are of great artistic value, such as those of Gu Kaizhi (345–406) of the Wei and Jin dynasty, Wu Daozi (active ca. 710–760) of the Tang dynasty, and Emperor Huizong (1082–1135) of Southern Song dynasty.

Sculptures and frescoes depicting deities in Daoist temples hold an important place in Chinese art history. Extant Daoist sculptural works from the 7th to 9th century include: a statue of the Heavenly Sage of Changyang, preserved in the Shanxi Provincial Museum; a statue of Laozi from the Tang Dynasty, preserved in the Shaanxi Provincial Museum; and statues of the Jade Maiden Spring Grotto, Mianyang City, Sichuan Province.

Sculptural works dating from the 11th to 14th century include: a monumental statue of Laozi at Qingliang Mountain, Chuanzhou, Fujian Province; the Grotto of Mount Shichuan in Sichuan; the Southern Mountain Grotto in Dazu, Sichuan; the handmaiden's statue of Holy Mother's Hall in Taiyuan, Shanxi; the statues in the Two Immortals Temple and Jade Emperor Temple in Jincheng, Shanxi; and the statues of the Three Pure Ones in Xuanmiao Temple in Suzhou, Jiangsu.

Statues dating from after the 14th century are the Dragon Mountain Grottoes in Taiyuan, Shanxi Province; the statue of the Water God Temple in Hongdong, Shanxi; the statues of the Twenty-Eight Constellations in Jincheng, Shanxi; the statues of Sacred Aunt Temple in Gaoping, Shanxi; and the statues of Guandi Temple in Jiezhou, Shanxi.

The most important Daoist temple frescos are those of the Eastern Sacred Mountain Temple in Tai'an, Shandong Province; the Northern Sacred Mountain Temple in Quyang, Hebei; Eternal Happiness Temple in Ruicheng, Shanxi; and the Water God Temple in Hongdong, Shanxi.

EMBROIDERED BANNERS DATING FROM THE QING DYNASTY HANG IN THE WHITE CLOUD TEMPLE, BEIJING.

These are all treasures of art of both China and the world. From November 2000 to January 2001, the Art Institute of Chicago hosted an exhibition titled "Taoism and the Arts of China" in Chicago and San Francisco. In it more than 150 items of Daoist sculpture and painting were exhibited, and more than 100,000 visitors attended. A symposium on the subject of Daoist art was held concurrently with the opening days of the exhibition.

Daoist music has greatly influenced Chinese classical music.

LAOZI RIDING A BLACK OX, BY MING DYNASTY ARTIST ZHANGLU.

Daoism inherited early musical themes, liturgical music and lyrics, as well as spells, charms, dances, and other music elements, plus bells, drums, and other instruments. The standard Daoist musical system started around the year 415, when Kou Qianzhi declared that he had been instructed by Master Lao to institute Daoist liturgies, and so published a *New Musical Liturgy of Commandments from the Clouds.* The rhythms he adopted, such as Huaxia anthems and Buxu chants, were adapted from the court music of Qin and Han dynasties. In later dynasties, Daoism continued to draw from

PERFORMANCE OF DAOIST LITURGICAL MUSIC, 2003.

court music, some compositions of which in fact were the works of famous Daoist emperors such as Tang Emperor Xuanzong and Song Emperor Huizong. Another important influence has been folk music of various regions in different periods. Thus there are some common rhythms, such as Shifang rhythms, followed by all temples, and some are local rhythms or airs, which are used only in temples in a given region, for example, Shaanxi rhythms, Beijing rhythms, and Wenzhou rhythms.

Daoist music is played in religious liturgies, and has specific uses as well as broad and profound philosophical meaning. It is closely related to folk customs and has always been popular among common people; it is thus a treasure house for the study of ancient and folk music of China. There have been three large-scale efforts aimed at collecting, editing, and studying Daoist music in the

Peoples' Republic: in 1950s these activities were mostly carried out in southeast China, from which emerged some important musical works such as the *Moon Reflected on the Second Springs,* well known as an *erhu* solo by a blind Daoist musician named Abing, as well as a number of important publications, including *A Report on Religious Music Survey in Hunan, An introduction to Daoist Music in Yangzhou* and a *Collection of Daoist Art in Suzhou.* During the 1970s and 80s the second research project worked intensively with sound, scores, charts, texts, and visual images, and studied historical changes, forms, and characteristics of Daoist music.

MONK PRACTICING BAGUA QUAN (EIGHT-TRIGRAM BOXING), A DAOIST MARTIAL ART.

In the 1980s, a third research project was conducted separately in Beijing, Shanghai, Suzhou, Wuhan, Mount Wudang, Mount Qianshan in Liaoning, and Mount Lao in Shandong, which produced many papers and recordings. In June of 1990, the TCI and the Music Institute of the Chinese Art Academy co-hosted a symposium on Chinese Daoist music. A Daoist orchestra later visited and performed in Venice, Florence, Rome, Toronto, Kuala Lumpur, Mali, Singapore, Hong Kong, and Taiwan, and held open concerts at the Beijing Odeum, all of which received praise from musical circles at home and abroad.

The Influence of Daoism on Folk Customs and Minorities

Daoism has always had a great influence on the daily life of Chinese people. Several of China's traditional holidays originated from Daoist practices, although their meanings have changed over the course of history.

The Festival of Lanterns—when families hang lanterns, eat dumplings, and attend lantern fairs—is currently celebrated on the fifteenth day of the first moon, bringing the New Year's holidays to a close. However, it was originally the Daoist holiday of Superior Principles Day, celebrated on the fifth day of the first moon, as prescribed by Daoist founder Zhang Daoling, and dedicated to the god of the Celestial Element. The custom of hanging lanterns and attending lantern fairs, as scholars of Song Dynasty have proved, was initiated by Han Emperor Wu as a way of offering sacrifices to the North Pole God (Taiyi) throughout the night of the fifteenth day of the first moon. Lanterns were used for this purpose, and the present custom is the synthesis of these two customs.

Tomb-Sweeping Day (Qingming Jie, literally the Pure and Shining Day), celebrated on the fourth day of the third moon, was transformed from Cold Food Day and No-Smoke Day, which, according to Song scholars, came from the story of Jie Zitui. Jie Zitui was a hermit of the Jin State during the Spring and Autumn period. He had performed great deeds for the state, but refused to become an official, instead remaining in the mountains. In order to force him to come out, the Duke of Jin decreed that the forests of the mountain where Jie lived be set on fire. But Jie Zitui preferred death by fire to obeying the Duke's request. When he heard this news, the Duke of Jin deeply regretted his actions and ordered all fires to be extinguished, and cold food to be eaten to memorialize this honorable sage. Jie Zitui was subsequently deified by Daoists because of his transcendent deeds. Annual memorial ceremonies held on the 105th day after the winter solstice were marked by putting out all fires, and hanging strings of date cakes threaded with wicker on door lintels. Today, however, it has become a day for families to sweep the tombs of their late relatives.

Dragon Boat Festival (Duanwu Jie or Duanyang Jie, literally the first five days of the middle summer), which falls annually on the

VISITORS TOUCHING A MONKEY SCULPTURE FOR GOOD LUCK DURING THE SPRING FESTIVAL AT WHITE CLOUD TEMPLE, BEIJING.

FAIR HELD DURING THE SPRING FESTIVAL, WHITE CLOUD TEMPLE, BEIJING.

fifth day of the fifth moon, was originally a Daoist holiday of exorcism. According to ancient texts, when this day arrived, each household pasted a piece of paper on its door with the image of the Celestial Master or a talisman "consecrated" with a red stamp in order to guard against any wandering ghosts or malevolent deities. In later times people came to associate this festival with the story of Quyuan, a loyal and patriotic minister of the state of Chu during the Spring and Autumn period, who drowned himself to demonstrate his own disappointment and disapproval of the ruling duke. People now throw rice dumplings into the water to memorialize Quyuan, or, in a variant version of the story, to feed the fish so that they do not eat him. In either case, it has become a day for making glutinous rice dumplings wrapped in bamboo or leaves.

A WESTERN DAOIST DISCIPLE IN MEDITATION ON MOUNT LU, JIANGXI PROVINCE.

The Mid-Autumn Festival, now held on the 15th day of the 8th moon, was originally a Daoist holiday for offering sacrifices to the Moon God, a practice inherited from early imperial sacrifices to the Moon God and celebrations of abundant harvests. Inspired by the poetic conceit that the moon is "round, like a cake," later generations have since adopted the custom of making and eating round pastries called "mooncakes" on this day.

The Double Ninth Festival is also called the Double Yang Festival because in Chinese thinking odd numbers correspond to *yang* (even numbers with *yin*) and the number nine is thus the largest single digit *yang* number. This festival is associated with the story of the Daoist priest, Fei Changfang, who saved the family of Huan Jing. Huan followed Fei to practice Daoist cultivation. One day Fei suddenly told Huan that his family would suffer from a great disaster, and instructed him to hurry home, bind garlands of *cornus officinalis* (*zhuyu* in Chinese, a kind of herb) around the arms of his family members, and take them to the top of a hill to drink chrysanthemum wine. Huan did as Fei instructed, and when the family returned home from the hill in the evening, they found all their domestic animals had died. Ever since then, it has become

a day of climbing mountains and drinking; women in the old days even donned bags of *cornus officinalis* to ward off evil spirits. Today this celebration has transformed into the Day of Climbing a Mountain; many elderly people climb a local hill and drink on this day, practices regarded as beneficial to their health and longevity; the day is consequently also called Elders' Day.

Moreover, the various customs of pasting pictures of gods on household doors, lighting firecrackers, and so on, typically originated from stories or beliefs related to Daoism.

Religious Daoism adopted many elements of minority beliefs and customs in the southwest China, including those of the Di, Qiang, Yu, Pu, Qiongmian, and Mosha people. For example, the central practice of "charmed water" probably came from witchcraft practices of these tribes. Conversely, after its foundation, the Daoist religion became the belief of many minorities. According to estimations, at least 10 million of 60 million people who are members of the 55 minorities of China maintain Daoist beliefs.

The Kitchen God is commonly worshiped in the families of the Achang nationality, whose home is in Yunnan; temples dedicated to the Jade Emperor, the Wall and Moat God, as well as Guandi can be found in the towns of the Achang people.

The Jing nationality, living in Guangxi, mostly worship the Daoist constellation gods, such as the Gods of the Sexagenary Cycle, the Thirty-Six Celestial Gods of the Big Dipper, and the Seventy-Two Earthly Gods of the Big Dipper. Daoist priests there belong to the Zhengyi denomination, who adhere to a father-to-son succession and do not live in monasteries.

The Maonan nationality, also inhabitants of Guangxi, believes in an eclectic religion that merges Daoist beliefs and customs with their tribal religion, called the Meishan Sect.

The Tu nationality, who live mainly in Qinghai, take the deity Zhenwu (the God of War, or Northern God) and the Empyrean Lady (or the Mystic Lady of the Highest Heaven) as their central focus of worship. They hold grand temple fairs on the Double Ninth Day every year for exorcisms and sacrificial ceremonies.

The Zhuang nationality, mostly living in Guangxi, also maintain many Daoist ideas along with their own ancient practices, and take Supreme Master Lao as the highest god, along with the Jade Emperor, the Three Pure Ones, Zhenwu, and the Empyrean Lady. As well, the Uigurs, the largest minority population of Xinjiang, originally practiced Daoism as their religion before adopting Islam.

THE INFLUENCE OF DAOISM ON
THOSE OUTSIDE OF CHINA

Over the past century, Daoism has spread to five continents along with various Chinese diaspora, mostly in the decades after 1940. Many non-Chinese have also begun to convert to Daoism in the late 20th century. According to an incomplete 1989 estimate by an international religious organization, there were Daoist believers or Daoist organizations in about 65 countries. According to Chinese scholar Zheng Tianxing's paper "Occidental Daoist Studies and the Spreading of Daoism in Foreign Countries," in nations outside of China, there were 31.28 million Daoist believers and more than 600 Daoist temples. Most of the Daoist activity was naturally in

WESTERN DAOIST MONKS PARADE FOR THE HEAVENLY SAGES.

DAOIST MONKS FROM SICHUAN PROVINCE PARTICIPATE IN THE CONSECRATION CEREMONY OF A STATUE IN MALAYSIA.

Asia, although there were estimated to be 25,000 believers and 54 temples in North America; 27,000 believers and 85 temples in South America; 29,000 believers and 98 temples in Europe; 3,400 believers and 54 temples in Africa; and 9,500 believers and 130 temples in Oceania. In Asia, there were 3,400 believers and 12 temples in Japan; 5,200 believers and 9 temples in Thailand, 2,700 believers and 7 temples in Burma; 820 believers and 4 temples in Indonesia; 120 believers and 2 temples in India; and 38,000 believers and 198 temples in Singapore.

The messages of Daoism—of naturalism, moderation, tolerance, benevolence, peace and goodwill—seem to have a broad and growing appeal, and we hope may yet constitute a precious gift from China to the wider world.